PRISONER
CELL BLOCK H
THE INSIDE STORY

PRISONER

Cell Block H

THE INSIDE STORY

Hilary Kingsley

Boxtree

First published in the UK 1990 by
BOXTREE LTD,
36 Tavistock Street,
London WC2E 7PB

1 3 7 9 10 8 6 4 2

Cover design by Paterson-Jones

Set and designed by Penny Mills
Printed and bound by the Bath Press, Avon

British Library Cataloguing in Publication Data
Kingsley, Hilary
"Prisoner Cell Block H": the inside story
1. Television drama series in English
I. Title
791.45
ISBN 1-85283-113-8

by the same author

Soap Box
Box of Delights
(with Geoff Tibballs)

Contents

Preface

This is a book for *Prisoner: Cell Block H* fans and all those interested in one of the great surprise success-stories of popular television. There were almost 700 one-hour episodes made, and the show is currently watched in 12 countries. It's a show millions watch and enjoy as a drama about a small community and the camaraderie and conflicts within it. Millions more enjoy it with their tongue firmly in cheek. Others claim its appeal is that it's the kind of television 'that's so bad it's good'. Others watch it because it focuses on women and lesbian relationships are featured without a great fanfare and without heavy moralising. For whatever reasons, around 10 million viewers in Britain lap up the series Australian television thought was history in 1986. No one connected with the production ever claimed it was art, and this book will not try to analyse its 'worth'.

As a viewer in the London region where the show until recently went out only once a week (when nothing more 'important' such as darts interupted it), I realise I know less than viewers in the Midlands and North and other ITV regions where many more episodes of the series have been shown. At least the 'On the Inside' section will not give away any secrets to other 'deprived' southern viewers.

My introduction is an attempt to place *Prisoner* on the map of Australian television. Chapter 1 covers the beginnings and teething troubles of the series, with comments from its creator, producers, writers and a designer.

Chapter 2, entitled 'On the Inside', is a collection of character-profiles and story-summaries with a few comments. Chapter 3 I've called 'On the Outside'. It contains the accounts of actresses and actors who worked on the show. I talked with most of them during a visit to Australia early in 1990. Some actresses were unavailable, so I have in places included comments from earlier interviews with reliable publications.

Chapter 4 is a light-hearted summing-up which includes a guide to 'Wentworth-speak' for non-addicts, some lines I class as gems, some notes on the *Prisoner* stage-play and the fan club, and a selection of what some celebrity fans think of the show.

And enjoy the photographs, for which we thank Grundy Television.

British viewers stay up late to follow Wentworth scenes like these

Introduction

Australia – Soap Centre of the World?

Something happened to British television in the late 1980s. With the spectacular success of *Neighbours* came a new interest, a new awareness. So many of the series we enjoyed – even if we didn't admit we ever watched them – and so many of the performers we liked came from Down Under.

From this side of the world it seemed as though everyone in the Australian television industry must suddenly have turned to soap opera. It is certainly true that *Neighbours, Home And Away, A Country Practice, Sons and Daughters, The Flying Doctors* and other long-running family serials have been among the most important drama productions made there. There is nothing new, though, about Oz soap. There have been about 40 of them to date, most highly popular at home, many very successful all round the world.

Soaps have always been a large part of their industry's output because, with America and Britain keen to export their expensively made drama series and Australia's population so small, there was little incentive for television network bosses to try to compete with remakes of the classics or expensive contemporary action series. The Australian feature-film makers were painting the wider landscapes.

So the job left to be done on the small screen was to reflect the small important things in Australian family life, to tell romantic stories which would strike chords with young viewers and comfort and amuse their mums.

What's fascinating about Australian soap opera is how it adapted to fill the gaps left by the British and American 'suppliers'. In the sixties the choice was between Britain's *Coronation Street*, loved for its quaintness and foreignness in some Australian cities (but gradually outstaying its welcome), and the American melodramas such as *Peyton Place*. At that time Australian producers were busily churning out police sagas; but two bright men, Don Cash and Bill Harmon, created *Number 96*, soap with sex and humour which still seems daring sixteen years later. Later Crawford Productions combined their skills for solid story-telling with cops and robbers and other keeping-the-rules series with scenes of home life. Then they chanced their luck with nostalgia, creating a saga of Australia's very special experiences of the war, *The Sullivans*.

Meanwhile the man who was to become 'the soapies' supremo', the 'pope of soap', Reg Watson, at Grundy Television, began to write about young love and to show how every society needs its gutsy women as a stabilising force. With *The Restless Years, Glenview High, The Young Doctors* and others Grundy rehearsed their skills for *Neighbours*, that most seductive and simple morality-tale of modern life.

By the mid-seventies, when nothing very inspiring was coming from Britain, and American soap was beginning its obsession with the mixed-up rich, greedy and beautiful, Watson looked to gaol and came up with *Prisoner*, about the mixed-up, poor and unlovely. It shouldn't have worked, but it did. It may have ended seven years later, but time may show that its hold on audiences outside Australia will outlive that of any of the softer soaps.

Certainly the Australians have not succeeded with a strong soap since. In the eighties, there were attempts to copy the Americans whose success with the super-rich sagas, *Dallas, Dynasty* and the many copies, seemed unstoppable. They came up with *Taurus Rising, Holiday Island, Possession*. But Aussie glitz never shone as brightly as the American stuff, and of Aussie hussies only neurotic Pat the Rat of *Sons and Daughters* stayed high on the hiss-lists. The Bitch, as Americans understood her, seemed sad, strange and out of place among laid-back Australians with their naturally sunny disposition and their admiration for the 'she'll be right, mate' optimism.

James Davern understood this difference in ideals when he began work on *A Country Practice*. This is soft soap full of rosy cheeks and quaint old country coves. Adultery doesn't exist in Wandin Valley;

the viewers wouldn't let it. But nevertheless this is drama which shows itself aware of real social problems which can't be solved between the opening music and the closing titles an hour later.

During the eighties policemen came back into soapland in Australia, but they weren't the harassed authority-figures of Homicide but husbands and wives, girlfriends and boyfriends with doubts and weaknesses. *The Flying Doctors* is not perhaps true soap (most of the stories are completed within an episode) but it's a descendant of all the medicated soaps since *Dr Kildare* proved that patients get better quicker if the doctors are handsome. This filmed series mixes adventure, illness and romance with shots of the sort of landscape they don't have in Dallas or Surrey. It's so successful in Europe and Scandinavia that Sydney Airport information assistants have lost count of the number of Danish and other backpackers arriving and asking directions to Cooper's Crossing.

In the past couple of years much has been written about the appeal of Australian shows to foreign audiences. Is it the sunny backdrop, the brightly dressed, straight-toothed, clear-skinned young characters so happy to fall in and out of love? Possibly it's the appeal of the Australian soap-houses, neither lavish American mansions nor Coronation Street two-up-two-downs, suggesting a comfortable, classless society (one where a plumber's family can afford the same fitted kitchen his neighbour the bank manager has).

None of these theories explains why

Prisoner works. It broke many of the usual rules about pretty young faces, nice homes, romance, romance and more romance. It was the strong-meat series which surprised everyone, Reg Watson's colleagues, the critics, and viewers who may not have thought they liked 'that sort of thing' but found they did. But, as *EastEnders* was to prove later, viewers can see through cuteness and when raw emotional conflict is on offer they love to join in the fight from their armchairs. When you think about it, a prison is an ideal setting for a soap. Here is a family, perhaps not a conventional one, but an enclosed society where people have to support each other to survive. The way Reg Watson saw his series, it was also an intriguing study of the way women suffer in a man's world. When it went to air early in 1979, it caused controversy, uproar in some quarters, but it was immediately successful. It was exported to America – where the title was changed to *Prisoner: Cell Block H*, to distinguish it from the (British) Patrick McGoohan drama series running there. In 1987 it was first shown in ITV regions to British audiences in a kamikaze slot, when all sensible folk should be tucked up. Any interest in it should have fizzled out in weeks. Yet around 10 million viewers here still stay up late to follow Wentworth Detention Centre's feisty gals. Other soaps claim bigger audiences, but *Prisoner* fans claim they are entertained in the fullest sense.

What *Prisoner* has, in abundance, is the important ingredient shared by all successful soaps, British, American and Australian: resilient, coping women who take what life throws at them and carry on.

In Australia's harsh and dangerous landscape, the early settlers struggled to survive. And it was the women of the isolated communities who pulled their families through. The women of Australian soap must have inherited their spirit. The late Pat McDonald, a veteran of several Australian soaps, was one who believed this. 'Australian women are not namby-pamby yet they're not devoid of feelings about men's ability, too', she said before her death in March 1990. 'They're strong because they have to be – some of them do the job of ten men. My own grandmother went into the desert. She lived hundreds of miles from the nearest town, there was no running water yet she grew vegetables in the dust. There were so many like her, some of them lived in canvas tents all their lives. Their strength was unbelievable.'

Another is Anne Charleston, who played Mum's daughter in *Prisoner* and now plays Madge, the coping woman of *Neighbours*. 'Madge isn't liberated- she's tough and aggressive because she needed to be with those great bullying brothers of hers. It doesn't occur to her that she shouldn't work. Most of the women in *Neighbours* work because they feel they have to – not to fulfil themselves.'

Former script editor of *The Flying Doctors*, Gwenda Marsh, echoes their views and adds that the heroine of Australian soap puts her American and British counterparts to shame. 'The American woman in soap is shown as a de-baller, the English heroine is a wimp saying, "Yes, love. No, love." But the Australian woman is finding a middle way. She's self-sufficient, no one is buying her ticket. Australian women hate to feel dependent.'

For someone used to British soap opera with its need to give a slice-of-life reality to plots, its tendency sometimes to be cynical, the Australian brands can seem sentimental, over-scented, especially in their lavish use of music to point up emotional moments. And it hasn't escaped our notice that an awf'lly-awf'lly English accent seems to be the number-one requisite for characters meant to be comical, snobbish or meddling. Perhaps Wentworth's Erica Davidson, that most refeened of prison governors, began it. Nosy Mrs Mangel, disapproving Aunt Edie and Cousin Hilary in *Neighbours* and the bossy matron in *A Country Practice*, all wickedly anti-pom, carried it on.

There's also no doubt that Australian writers understand better than others young women's ideas of romance, their need to feel accepted. They understand the older woman's frustrations with her children and her need to know she's a good 'un in the eyes of her neighbours.

Today Australian actors and film crews are probably the most productive in the world. Soaps are made so fast an actress can be pregnant on a Tuesday and hold a baby in her arms two months later. With only three commercial home networks, the television industry there has to be fiercely competitive, and series have to be long-running to be cost-effective and saleable. So an output of 92 hours

of *Prisoner* a year, or 115 hours of *Neighbours* (compared with around 20 hours in Britain and America) is not unusual.

It's a formula that seems to be effective – hence Britain's delight at the invasion of the new wizards of Oz and what seems to some the Aussification of the world. In Holland children under five are already speaking ''Strine' because of their addiction to Aussie soaps. *Neighbours* and *Home and Away* delight huge audiences, mainly of teenagers, all over Europe. The most frequent complaint received by Central Television, the station serving Britain's Midlands where *Prisoner: Cell Block H* is screened three times a week, is the protest that the show's time has been changed. Alternatively there is a barrage of bitterness from viewers each time a sporting event such as snooker wipes out an episode. Carol Warburton, Central's press officer who deals with the series, said: 'I can't think of another show where the audience is so passionate.'

Prisoner has been shown in 12 countries including America, Thailand and Trinidad.

Yet the people who make Aussie soap work, the actors, are not garlanded with praise, and few have reaped great rewards. They pay a heavy penalty for their success because soap opera is often sneered at by Australians, who consider it fodder, 'lowest common denominator' programming. (Mind you, they have been used to several

Opposite Judith Bryant (Betty Bobbit) in trouble with Erica Davidson (Patsy King)

Sheila Florance, Val Lehman and Colette Mann

Meg Jackson (Elspeth Ballantyne) and Vera Bennett (Fiona Spence)

low-budget American day-time soaps which are hard to defend on any level.) In Britain it's acceptable, even fashionable, to admit to enjoying one or more of the soaps. It's 'in' among the educated young. Not so yet in Oz. Although soapie series are top of the ratings in Melbourne, Sydney and in many other cities (only major sporting fixtures beat them), it tends to be the very young who admit to watching them. Aussie soap addicts are yet to come out of their closets. So for the average soap actor the hard work and ballyhoo can (and usually do) mean little recognition as an artist, only a modest amount of money, and can be followed by long periods of obscurity and unemployment. This was certainly the case with many of the actresses who helped *Prisoner* win over 20 awards during its home run.

Yet, with lower budgets and more hastily written scripts, it's clear that Australian actors try perhaps harder than others to make their story-lines take wing. Gwenda Marsh used to tell her writers and actors: 'If you don't mean to treat your soapie like the next production for the Royal Shakespeare Company – don't do it.' The women who served time in Wentworth didn't need to be told.

LANDMARKS IN AUSTRALIA'S SOAP OPERA HISTORY

1958	*Autumn Affair*
1967	*Bellbird* (to 1977)
1968	*Motel* (closed that year)
1972	*Number 96* (to 1977)
1973	*Certain Women*
1974	*The Box* (to July 1977)
1974	*Class of 74/75*
1975	*The Young Doctors* (to 1981)
1976	*The Sullivans* (to March 1983)
1977	*The Restless Years* (to 1980)
1977	*Cop Shop* (to July 1984)
1977	*Glenview High* (to 1979)
1979	*Prisoner* (to 1986)
1979	*Skyways* (to 1981)
1980	*Arcade*
1981	*A Country Practice* (to present day)
1981	*Punishment*
1981	*Sons and Daughters* (to 1987)
1982	*Holiday Island*
1982	*Taurus Rising* (to 1983)
1982	*Waterloo Station*
1983	*Carson's Law* (to December 1984)
1985	*Possession*
1985	*Neighbours* (to present day)
1986	*Prime Time* (to January 1987)
1986	*The Flying Doctors* (to present day)
1988	*Richmond Hill* (to 1989)
1988	*Home and Away* (to present day)
1988	*All the Way*
1989	*E-Street*
1989	*GP*
1989	*The Power, the Passion*
1990	*Family and Friends*

1
AUSSIE TV GOES TO GAOL

Rita Connors (Glenda Linscott) under police escort

Picture page 16 Bea Smith (Val Lehman) shows Lyn Warner (Kerry Armstrong)
who is boss, while Vera Bennett (Fiona Spence) looks on

THE KEY TO WENTWORTH

Ask anyone who has ever caught snatches of *Prisoner: Cell Block H* what he or she remembers. Tough women in denim dungarees, some with beer-bellies, broken noses, permanent snarls, the sound of shouting, brawling, tugging each other's hair, trapping hands in a steampress, bashing someone by the huge tumble-drier, knifings, shootings, poisonings, kidnappings, group loyalties, lesbian relationships...

Not what you'd call a pretty sight. But different. As bright actress Glenda Linscott, who won a Best Actress award for her work in it, said: ' *Prisoner* was outrageous. It was outrageous that we made it and outrageous that people watched and go on and on watching.'

Yet anyone who has been to Australia knows that people there are not so unlike us. Australia is not a land teaming with antisocial women, women who break the law and are prone to violence. In 1979 there were just over 300 women in Australian gaols compared with nearly 9,500 men. That means men in custody outnumbered women by about thirty to one – roughly the same proportion as in Britain. Most of us never meet a woman who has been 'banged up' for fiddling money from her firm, let alone one who has committed a robbery or inflicted grievous bodily harm on another. That's why a television serial about such 'oddities' is likely to fascinate a fair few of us. Whether it's a voyeuristic fascination or a genuine interest in society's misfits, it's hard not to be curious.

How do women end up in prison and how do they manage when they get there? Reg Grundy was the Australian television boss who decided the late 1970s was a time to make drama about this minority. Ten years earlier, this former boxing commentator had formed the Grundy Organisation from his flat in Elizabeth Bay, Sydney, selling one show, *Wheel of Fortune*, which is still in production today. Thirty years later his international company can claim to have produced more hours of television than any other independent company in the world. Last year they were making over 40 hours a week and during most weeks they fill about 17 hours on British television. Reg Grundy has created and made over 80 quiz and game shows and 22 drama series of which *Prisoner* is one of his most spectacularly successful. But back in the 1970s the idea looked anything but promising until Reg Grundy asked Reg Watson, his vice-president in charge of drama, to make it work.

Watson, a softly spoken Queenslander, wrote his first play when he was 13 and produced it for the stage in his native Brisbane when he was 18. He acted, wrote and produced plays for the Brisbane Repertory Theatre and worked in radio until he could afford his first trip to Britain in the 1950s. Over here, he worked for the BBC as an actor, then joined Lew Grade's Birmingham-based ATV company helping Lew Grade and Val Parnell with their variety and game shows.

Drama was his first love, though, and by 1964 he had created *Crossroads,* the inimitable motel saga which Lew Grade thought would last 10 years. Reg predicted merely a few. It lasted for 24 years. He wrote, directed, produced and edited it with unflagging dedication for 10 years. Then in 1973 he suddenly yearned for the sun and the bright colours of home and booked a trip which was to alter the course of Australian television history.

Reg went to work for Reg Grundy and helped him expand from games and quizzes to drama. As an ideas man, a writer and producer he seems to have been a power-house. His long-running serials included *The Young Doctors*, *Sons and Daughters*, *The Restless Years* and *Neighbours*, all great successes, and one or two flops. Then Reg Grundy explained his women's-gaol idea. Reg Watson said: 'He said he'd always wanted to do a prison one, but I thought it would be incredibly depressing – mainly because I knew nothing at all about the subject. If you just take a lot of tough women and put them behind bars, the novelty wears off quickly. So I went to the Corrective Service Department and they put me in touch with a wide cross-section of women prisoners and women warders. Someone introduced me to a woman who had spent twelve years inside. She was beautifully turned out, stately, with neat grey hair and very genteel. She didn't smoke or drink. She had been found guilty of killing three men but she hadn't done it, she told me,' he went on with a wry chuckle. 'In fact, when I started to talk to women inside, I found everyone was innocent!'

Watson and his researchers spent nine months visiting institutions, talking to people inside and outside and ploughing through Royal Commissions into prisons. A couple of women wardens were regularly consulted over story-lines. Wentworth, said Watson, is probably a combination of Silverwater women's prison in New South Wales and Fairlea gaol in Melbourne. 'We combined the rules and regulations of both places, but perhaps our security systems aren't so good. We took dramatic highlights, but in some cases we had to tone down the characters and incidents. Some of the people were just too violent and the events too shocking. But it was never in our minds to make it a knocking series. If there were warders who were sadistic bitches, that's because the people we spoke to told us there were warders like that. We've relied on advice from prison people in everything.

'We came up with episodes which shocked people when they were seen in America. It was shown at peak time in Los Angeles and at first a group of lesbians picketed the studio. I can remember frantically telexing LA, trying to explain that the scripts were not anti-lesbian. They had to watch on, see how things turned out. They did, and Franky Doyle became a figurehead. When she died they held a wake.'

Watson liked Franky very much. 'I'd based her on a real woman I'd talked to. Very tough but clearly vulnerable underneath. And the actresses really excelled. We had so many experienced performers falling over themselves to get parts, it was extraordinary. But, then, most actresses were used to serving tea on television.'

Reg Watson never claimed that *Prisoner*

Prisoner presented life in Wentworth with no holds barred

was the whole truth about prison life. 'The most important thing is to entertain. We weren't trying to preach; it wasn't meant to be a documentary. Anyway, it would have been deadly dull if we'd tried to make it absolutely realistic,' he said. 'There would have been rows of women sitting around doped and depressed. We made it like a girls' boarding school gone wrong with lots of practical jokes which sometimes led to violence. We suggested tension and occasionally dealt with sexual relationships.'

Former teacher Peita Lechford was one of the researchers who helped Reg Watson and his writers. Not only did she observe and talk to a wide range of women inmates of gaols, to learn personal stories, understand how the Queen Beas were selected, pecking orders formed and followed, and what happened when they weren't; she was also able to draw diagrams for the set-designers and describe the insides of cells.

She confirmed that women had chances to vary what they wore, to work outside, have contact with the outside world and to interact with male prisoners. In one gaol, she said, 'men do the cooking and there's a ritual as a procession of a group of male prisoners escorted by guards walk up to the women's kitchen and one by one dump the food. The women catcall, whistle and make sexual comments about the guys.' She also noted that a high proportion of women prisoners were fat because boredom seemed an inescapable problem and it was hard not to count the minutes between meal-breaks.

IRON BARS DO NOT A PRISON MAKE

Work started on *Prisoner* in the autumn of 1978 in the ATV Channel 10 studios in Nunawading, a grassy, sparsely populated region about 20 miles from the city of Melbourne, the same studios which now house the sets of Ramsay Street, setting for the cleaner-than-clean *Neighbours*. Thousands of dollars were spent converting part of the exterior of the studio's office building to make it look like a prison-block. Brick cladding and false bar-covered windows were put up. What was a security fence was covered in brick cladding to make it look like an outside prison-wall. Innocent deliverymen were frequently seen at the studio gates, scratching their heads, sure they'd gone astray and ended up 'in pokey'.

In the grounds – which had once been an orchard and were still tended by the former owner – a vegetable garden was laid out. Real vegetables began to grow, though no thanks to Doreen and Lizzie and the other inmates soon to be seen working there. (In fact one critic pointed out that she had yet to see more feeble rows of plants. The answer must be that, because Wentworth's lack of exercise facilities made Strangeways look luxurious, this garden doubled as a recreation spot and the vegetation was trampled underfoot.)

Back to the start. An old gate that used to fence off a piece of land became the gate that fenced off the prison farm, and another patch of lawn became the prison barbecue area. Mostly, though, the famous Melbourne sun, which seems to have the strength of a 40-watt bulb, made outdoor meals fairly grim affairs. Inside studio B a $1.5 million computerised lighting system was installed for use exclusively on this series. At first twelve permanent sets were made, but later, according to director then producer Philip East, sets doubled. 'The dining-room and the recreation-room were one and the same with bookcases put in and taken out,' he said. The cells were never a problem. What was a headache were the corridors. The long, echoing walkways viewers see so often were a sham. He said: 'We had only one L-shaped section with wooden walls which we dressed and re-dressed, putting in and taking out door units and bar units. The actresses had to walk through, stop while we changed things, then start again. It was a bind and a bit of a joke when we had to do it so many times.'

The look of Wentworth Detention Centre has been mocked by some British viewers, who *insist* that they can see all the walls wobble and that there is no glass in the windows. Actress Patsy King jokes that all the tunnels dug by the prisoners must have weakened the foundations. Producer Phil East says the critics need their eyes tested. East, who took over from Ian Bradley to become the second producer of the series, went on: 'When they started the series they decided it should be set in a modern prison and, yes, the sets did lack the character of an older building. This was emphasised by the British prison drama *Within These Walls* which was running here at the same time. But the sliding gates were metal and very heavy, many of the walls were the solid walls of the studio buildings and only the cell doors were wooden. When they were slammed the sound wasn't authentic, so we added sound effects on. We were working 48 weeks of the year, making two hours of drama a week and on a limited budget, so at times the appearance may not have been brilliant; it wasn't easy, but I think it was adequate.'

What had been easy was the casting. In place of the offers, turn-downs, new offers to new people, the delays, headaches, bargaining and changes which usually occur with major television productions, almost every actress offered a part accepted. The reason was that this was a long-awaited chance for actresses. All the leading roles were for women, and women of all ages, all shapes and sizes. Australian actresses who weren't young, whose faces weren't their fortunes, fell over themselves to be part of it, so rare was it that a soap's scripts did not require most of the characters to 'get their gear off' and prance around a swimming-pool. And the roles of murderers, armed robbers, poisoners or con-women were obviously more meaty than those they were usually offered: housewives and mums.

Ian Bradley, first producer of *Prisoner*, recalls: 'It was International Year for Women, women were beginning then to examine their roles in society, and the basic idea behind the series was that many women were prisoners of the system whether in gaol or not. Reg Watson had written it as a 16-part self-contained series. But when we started screening we realised we were on to a winner.' One sign of this was that the Network bosses, having seen a few episodes, immediately ordered a further forty-two. The show's first 12-month stretch was assured.

A part of its instant success was the pretty theme-song, 'On the Inside', recorded by Lynne Hamilton. Lancashire-born Lynne started singing at 14 and toured England in a rock group, the Desperadoes, a supporting act to such artists as Eric Burdon and the Animals and Freddie and the Dreamers. She later formed the Caravelles, who had a hit with 'You Don't Have to Be a Baby to Cry', toured Europe and met superstars such as Jimi Hendrix and the Rolling Stones. 'We made a few hit records but the group split up, so I came to Sydney with my family in 1975 and started again.'

In 1979 she was asked to record the *Prisoner* theme-song, which was a moderately successful single there. But in 1989 it was relaunched in Britain and zoomed to number three in the charts. The record company had by then lost touch with Lynne, now married to her manager Greg Dilanian and living in Melbourne. But news filtered Down Under, and Lynne made a trip home tickled pink by her born-again hit record. In the mean time, she reported, she had received thousands of letters from prisoners and their families. 'I've never been inside a prison, but now I've proved I'm not dead I'm being asked to visit gaols to give concerts. It's fantastic.' Fans were delighted when the song once blared out of a radio in one of the houses in *Neighbours*.

Phil East, producer of *Prisoner* for two years, says it was a uniquely fast-moving operation. 'The actresses did not spend the usual time in make-up or having their hair done and there were rarely any delays deciding on clothes. For one thing, the women spent 90 per cent of the time in their prison uniforms. I remember the actresses used to urge the writers to give them scenes when they could dress up or at least have a change, but those scenes were sparingly done. In many ways the story lines and scripts were the hardest area. We were also very concerned with the level of violence. We showed prisoners murdering, burning hands in the steam-press, fighting. We had someone impaled on a spike – but we decided not to show it. There was a danger in becoming too

graphic; that wasn't the intention.'

The writing, the acting, and producing the violence for one and then two hours a week became exhausting. Early on most of the action revolved around Franky Doyle, a nicotine-stained lesbian bikie inside for armed robbery and played by bright Brisbane actress Carol Burns, the show's first new star. In one scene Franky and her pals went berserk in the library. It terrified at least one of the extras so much she was found under a table, sobbing. Carol said she came out of the recording with hands shaking, vision blurred.

It was easy to sense the tension, and the producers made sure individual performers had breaks between such scenes. In time, according to many, the actresses became like their characters. One actress recalled how the dressing-room was for a time a tunnel which all members of the cast had to share. Amusingly the actresses playing the crims tended to use one side and those playing the screws used the other. Because the space was so cramped, they often became quite aggressive to each other, assuming the characteristics of their 'them' and 'us' roles. Marie Trevor, the producer who took over from East, said: 'It became a strain. It was hard on the writers too. Every day they had to dream up a way for one of these unsavoury women to kill or take revenge on another. We had to keep the violence down.'

But *Prisoner* remained a Tuesday- and Thursday-night treat for Australian viewers. Phil East recalled: 'When the Network decided to end *Prisoner* after 692 episodes in 1986, there was a huge protest.'

THE FIRST WOMAN OF WENTWORTH

One reason *Prisoner* was a winner, according to many of the actresses, was the quality of the scripts, especially the earlier scripts written by Denise Morgan. Yet Denise herself was surprised and doubtful about the series when Reg Watson first outlined it.

She said: 'When Reg Watson showed me his draft of the first two scripts I said, "It's a bit ugly, isn't it?" It seemed a bit risqué for Australian television, so unlike anything that had gone before. I told him, "I don't know if the audience will stand for this. They're used to clean-livers, mother figures."

'But Reg didn't see it as that much of a departure. And later on I saw that in some ways he was right. Anyway, he was very serious about it, and we got down to work and wrote it together. Initially there were to be only sixteen to twenty episodes on the 10 Network and with an ending – Karen Travers was to be proved innocent. The network then decided they wanted more, so we had to change the stories and turn it from a maxi-series into a serial. Karen had to stay a lot longer.

'We were helped in our research by a terrific woman who had been inside, and a number of the characters were based on real people. "Mum", for instance, was based on an elderly woman who had been inside, and had later set up a refuge for ex-prisoners. Others we devised to balance and contrast or for light relief.

'We wrote the characters as survivors, and I think that was the show's secret even if it wasn't obvious. The reason it took off so well at first was that people were astounded to see women who could use their fists to protect themselves, women who could be violent. Personally I loved Doreen and Lizzie. They started out as humorous characters but became firm fixtures and quite serious at times. I also gave Vera Bennett her nickname "Vinegar Tits" – Fiona Spence has never forgiven me. I liked her – she was not corrupt, she was tough on everybody including herself.

'Franky was another one I adored – this boiler-suited heavy dyke who showed her softer side with her brother. I had the job of writing Franky out when Carol Burns wanted to leave. She objected to the show going out two hours a week instead of one; she feared they couldn't maintain the same standard, there'd be too many compromises.

'As the series progressed we introduced many subjects which were controversial, but I was always very cautious with drugs because I knew a lot of schoolkids were watching in Australia when it was seen at 8.30. Kids were mimicking the characters in school. I made Bea Smith very anti-drugs, and I tried to have pregnancy portrayed responsibly.

'I left after about 200 episodes – I feared my brain would go dead if I didn't. But I look back on *Prisoner* as something special and something important.'

Since leaving, Denise has written scripts for *A Country Practice, The Sullivans, An Indecent Obsession, The Flying Doctors* and a new Australian series, *Embassy.*

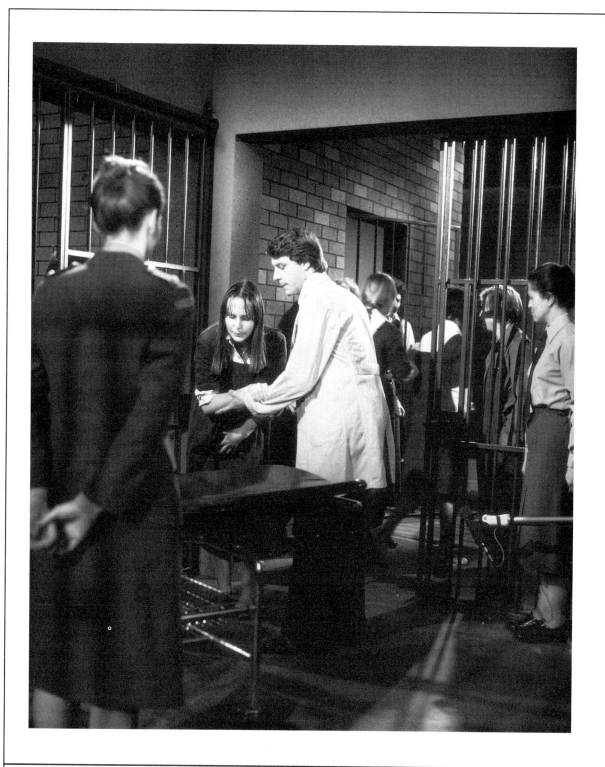

IAN SMITH, now famous as funny, huffing Harold Bishop in *Neighbours,* served a hard seven-year stretch as script editor of *Prisoner: Cell Block H.* And for four of those he did double porridge – playing Ted Douglas, Head of Corrective Services, as well.

'It was the only time I've ever written for myself,' said the 51-year-old star who first stepped on stage as a baritone in *The Desert Song.* 'I write episodes of *Neighbours* but I can't bear to write for Harold. If I think of any jokes for him, I feel the other actors might resent me giving myself the best lines, so the only times I tried it was very flat. Also I feel that actors should have the right to criticize the script, and I don't like to inhibit that. If, having written it, I was in the same scene, it might cause the actors to hold back about something they don't feel right with. And with *Prisoner* it became too much, so I had the pleasure of writing myself out – although it wasn't killing myself off. That might have been painful.

'In the early stages I had my backside kicked a few times,' he said. 'I wrote what I thought were dramatic action scenes, the producers stopped me and I disagreed violently. It was part of my learning process in production. Looking back I see that they were right, but I hated sacrificing a great piece of drama just because it might have been contentious had it gone to air. I found out that we were watched by schoolchildren who were adopting our characters' names such as Queen Bea and

Opposite Wentworth's doctor, Greg Miller (Barry Quin) in the thick of things

Vinegar Tits and emulating the people in the show. We had to send some of the actresses out to talk to children in schools to push home the message that this was *not* real life, it was only a piece of entertainment. Sometimes things became so serious that we had to give them little lessons – I used to hate doing this, because I think if you have a message you use Telecom; we're entertainers not educators.

'It was also a very popular show in prisons, so we knew that if we handled any matter irresponsibly we could have caused serious riots. We actually found that in one prison the top dog adopted the name Queen Bea.'

After his early wrangles with his bosses, Ian's problems switched. He had to deal with the 'deep throats' among the real prisoners and warders who fed him juicy tales from their experiences – these led to many of the stories in the series – and also with disappointed writers and some cast members who wanted to 'let go' with more daring sequences. It didn't make him popular.

'I was not liked as head editor because I had to step on so many stories,' he said. 'It was very difficult to keep coming up with new ideas. We went through the whole shooting library – hunger strikes, inmate revolts, industrial action by warders, a quarantine, arson, abortion, a woman who gave birth in her cell. We had to be very careful about using the snippets of information people gave us because we knew they were often biased one way or another and we had to take the middle road.'

Amateur theatricals from Doreen Burns (Colette Mann) and Lizzie Birdsworth (Sheila Florance)

Ian can smile now at the incidents that were 'blamed' on the series, though at the time the complaints were treated seriously. 'For argument's sake, there was a fire at Fairlea women's prison when two inmates were burnt to death. Unfortunately one of our episodes which went to air two weeks later had a very similar story-line and we were accused of capitalising on the anguish of these real victims. But, for God's sake, we had made that segment almost four months before the Fairlea incident. We still copped the abuse, though.'

On another occasion the cast was filming in a building when they heard the loud sound of sirens and saw the police helicopter hovering nearby in a stakeout. Only later did they learn that a former prisoner who had assisted with plots for the story-line had been shot dead in a confrontation with police. He was killed trying to hijack a security truck carrying $1.8 million.

Ian is the first to admit that life in Wentworth was not like real life 'inside'. He said: 'If we'd had to portray the real thing, we'd have lasted only a week. It's true horrific things happen, but they're over and done with in seconds. That would never do for television. The thing about prison life is that the tiniest problem is magnified. If I leant towards you and reached for your coffee-cup, you'd think nothing much of it. It wouldn't be a threat. In prison that cup, that possession, is yours; you may have done some graft for it. It may only be a plastic cup, but you'd defend it like mad.'

Ian added his admiration for the cast. The sheer drabness of the gaol surrounds and prison fatigues sparked fine performances from many of them, he believed. 'They had to be great actresses,' he said. 'There weren't any props or great costumes to pull them through. It was facial expressions, feel, timing that brought *Prisoner* to life.'

And, of course, there were mishaps. The steam-press was not real – not surprisingly; the steam came from a steam-bottle which pumped out clouds of vapour, but the press was safely cool. But there was a lurking danger – an escaped snake.

'We used a snake in one of the stories. It was supposed to have bitten Meg; she went to hospital, and the creature was eventually caught and killed. Only it wasn't really. It was a dangerous variety – a yellow something, I forget which –

which had been de-fanged. It was brought in for the scene, let out of its box, and after we did the scene it vanished. They searched everywhere, but it was never found. From then on it wasn't a very comfortable feeling knowing that somewhere in your workplace a dangerous reptile is lurking. I don't believe they ever saw it again. They used a model for the dead snake, of course.'

But most of the action scenes were fun, Ian recalled. Especially one when a riot had to take place in the kitchens. 'A food fight was going at full pelt, and they had quite enough of it on film, but none of the cast heard the word "cut" so they went on slapping cream pies all over the place and at each other. It was hilarious. When they finally stopped the set was a shambles. In the end they had to take it all apart, clean everything and make it up all over again.'

When *Prisoner* ended, Ian did not relish his 'freedom'. 'I was very, very upset,' he said. 'I know it sounds dumb, but I was so wrapped up in that show. But I don't think I would ever do it again. You can't go back. It's like going to a school reunion. You get too much of a shock when you see these old, bald, red-nosed fellows you once knew as callow youths.'

FIRST REACTIONS

The serial began to be shown in February 1979, and audiences were soon transfixed. But, first, *Prisoner* had to undergo a baptism of fire. Several critics were clearly stunned by the fruity language and tough action. One delicate (male) critic called

Wentworth 'a Hell house of appalling animalistic behaviour' where 'morality is a mockery'. The governor of Victoria's Fairlea prison, Miss Wanda Miller, objected because she thought the serial was a reflection on practices in her prison. Some prison officers took umbrage, claiming that they weren't like beastly Bennett & Co. The Festival of Light's Fred Nile railed against the 'illicit sex acts', the language and the violence, and some viewers were rather sniffy about Franky Doyle. A few prisoners chipped in, too – they protested that life in Wentworth was not realistic because it wasn't boring enough. But the viewing figures rose steadily and the show was soon a favourite in Sydney where citizens traditionally reject anything that comes from the rival city, Melbourne.

But, if critics can make or break productions on stage, they have a harder job telling people what to watch in their own home. The series was the second most popular show in the 1979 National Top Ten. (A year later it was still in the chart but at number eight.)

Perhaps the show's greatest triumph was in August 1979 when viewers on the West Coast of America were shown a two-hour introduction before the serial began in a peak-time weekly slot. Despite the fact that Americans knew none of the stars, the show captured a quarter of the viewers – and there were seven channels. Screened on the KTLA Channel 5, it stole audiences from the two big networks, NBC and CBS, and was beaten only by ABC which was showing the then well-established hit series *Charlie's Angels*.

No American peak-time series had featured lesbian characters. None has since, and even 'daring' British soaps such as *East Enders* and *Brookside*, which have acknowledged the existence of gay men, have shied away from the portrayal of gay women. Australian viewers had already shown an acceptance of homosexuality. In their outrageous 1972 soap *Number 96*, one of the main 'goodies' was a gay solicitor, Don Finlayson, whom many of the women characters tried to 'convert'. And there was hardly a ripple when another series *The Box* featured a bisexual character, played by Judy Nunn, who took the role of Joyce Martin in *Prisoner* and is now a star of *Home and Away*. Phil East said, 'The lesbianism was never shown as anything surprising. It was part of the possessiveness you'd expect to develop in prison.'

Reg Watson was naturally gratified when the initial hoo-ha died down and *Prisoner* became a solid favourite with viewers. But there were no doubts about the wisdom of ending it seven years later. 'We ended it not because we ran out of ideas; we never had a problem thinking of material. But we felt it had run its course; it was heavy-going for everyone. We could never do it again. We tried to do something similar a few years later; we tried a male version called *Punishment*. Mel Gibson was in an early episode. But it didn't work at all. There was no mystique. People knew more or less how men coped without women, they knew what they do as far as sex is concerned, and they didn't want to see unrelieved violence.'

Women teachers of Australia did not

Rita Connors (Glenda Linscott) and Lorelei Wilkinson (Paula Duncan)

lament the ending of the series. They had inherited the nicknames of the screws, notably 'Vinegar Tits', thanks to the show's devoted younger audience. *Prisoner* had saved Australia's Network 10 from a downhill slide (a list of failures such as *Tea Ladies*, *Hotel Story* and *The Bluestone Boys* had preceded the opening of Wentworth's gates). It had renewed Reg Watson's reputation and helped make reputations for Phil East who (like Marie Trevor after him) went on to produce *Neighbours*.

Most important, *Prisoner* gave actresses who might otherwise have been seen only pouring tea a real chance to act. The roles they played made soap history. Here are some of them.

2
ON THE
INSIDE

Joan 'The Freak' Ferguson is in command

Picture page 32 Franky Doyle (Carol Burns)

BELLA ALBRECHT, played by Liddy Clark, was the mystery prisoner whisked into solitary in the early hours. She'd been besotted with a man, but he would not marry her because she had a five-year-old child. So she'd murdered the child and mutilated his body to try to prevent his being identified. They'd put her into solitary for her own protection, and although she was soon let out she was kept away from the other prisoners. Davo ordered the confiscation of the telly and all the radios so that the other women should not learn the truth. It came out, of course. Davo blamed Karen Travers and suspended her attendance at 'uni'. In fact twisted psychologist Peter Clements had given Bea the details.

Big Martha Eves cornered Bella in the showers but, far from wishing her harm, only wished to be her friend and offered to help her escape. Martha even had a plan; but as it involved a wooden horse and a tunnel – she'd seen it in a film – Bella was less than impressed. But she saw the advantage in having such hefty protection and pretended to be friendly while being under no illusions about Martha's brainpower ('She's all right to keep the heavies at bay, but you'd get more sense from an orang-utan').

The real threat came from Monnie, who was scornful of the way that the other women were pussyfooting around the issue. She tried to throttle Bella. Martha rushed to the rescue. Monnie got twenty-four hours in solitary. But Bella made the mistake of calling Martha a cretin. The result was that Martha strangled Bella in the washroom and was carted off to a more secure prison.

VERA BENNETT, played by Fiona Spence, was the tough 'Vinegar Tits', the Miss Nasty of Wentworth. The nickname was very apt: she lacked almost every touch of humanity. Vera's life had been blighted by the demands of her invalid mother. By the time the old woman died it was too late for Vera to change. Cold, lonely, not loved by anyone – her brief moments of affection seemed always to turn sour – only when making the prisoners' lives hell was she fulfilled.

Vera was Wentworth's deputy governor and missed no opportunity to undermine Davo's authority, with the intention of taking her job. But when prison discipline seemed to be about to collapse, and the future of Davo's governorship was in doubt, the Prison Department decided that the Wentworth regime needed a strong male hand, so Jim Fletcher was brought in as deputy governor and Vera was *demoted*.

From time to time she tried to find true love. A local cop wined and dined her a couple of times, but soon lost interest. When Vera finally thought she had found it, with George Lucas, the man turned out to be a drug-dealer, and Vera came close to serving time herself. (He left her tied up in her flat as he made his escape.) Then she thought she'd found a soulmate in Jock Mackay. They dined by candle-light and discussed tightening prison discipline. But Jock was a crook – Vera spotted him receiving a backhander – and Vera was essentially honest, so the relationship came to nothing. She even failed to find affection with a lost dog; she bought it a basket and toys, but soon afterwards the owner reclaimed the dog while Vera was taking it for a walk in the park. (She kept this compassionate episode secret, so the women were convinced that she'd had the dog put down.)

Like Davo, Vera was obsessed with Bea Smith. Like Davo, too, she never came out on top. She thought the women scarcely human, and her only pleasure came from believing that her prejudices had been justified. Naturally she opposed all attempts to bring in educational projects or work schemes, and gloated when such initiatives came to grief. She had the honour of calling off the factory project when Noelene Bourke was implicated in the theft of bolts of cloth. Davo's instruc-

tion that the women should be taken back to Reynolds's factory and allowed to continue only reinforced Vera's views about Davo's incompetence.

Vera's doubts about the factory pro-gramme proved well founded: union rep Hazel Crow told her about Reynolds's plan to use the women on non-govern-ment work and threatened strike action if this was not stopped. Vera enjoyed telling Davo that Reynolds was a crook. Unfortunately Davo – blinded by love – decided to let the work project continue. She soon regretted it, when Kay White was arrested for stealing the factory's pay-roll and was remanded to Wentworth. Vera reported Davo's connection with Reynolds to the Department, and an inquiry was ordered.

The arrival of the folksy Agnes Forster as the new social worker upset Vera ('If it was up to me, I'd dispense with social workers altogether').

Kay White wasn't slow to appreciate Vera: 'You're the vilest thing I've ever met,' she said.

LIZZIE BIRDSWORTH, played by Sheila Florance, was wily and wizened, truly one of the wonders of Wentworth. The comic relief of the series, usually as part of a double act with Doreen, seventy-two-year-old Lizzie considered herself 'a dab hand with poisons' and had served twenty years for poisoning four shearers – although this hadn't disqualified her from work in the prison kitchen. But after she had spent all that time behind bars fresh evidence revealed that, although at the time everyone – including Lizzie herself –

Lizzie Birdsworth (Sheila Florance) makes her feelings known. Doreen Burns (Colette Mann) has heard it all before

had believed that she poisoned the men, she had not in fact been responsible for their death. She was released and was promised a lot of compo.

There were two endearing things about her. One was her addiction to grog and cigarettes. She occasionally made her own booze, but also helped herself to the sickbay's surgical alcohol and Davo's drinks-cabinet and accepted the smuggled stuff. The other was her bad heart. This proved invaluable when a diversion was required.

While the staff crowded round Lizzie, the other women got on with whatever they had planned. Lizzie's frailty ceased to be a joke for a while when old Edith Wharton was remanded to Wentworth on a vagrancy charge, was put in Lizzie's cell and died in her sleep. Faced with evidence of her own mortality, Lizzie was subdued for a while afterwards. She feigned a 'religious conversion' – it took the form of singing hymns at the top of her voice at night and ticking the women off for their wicked ways – in the hope of being allowed out of prison to attend Sally Army shindigs.

Once her name had been cleared, she was released into the care of the halfway house, where her pal Doreen was already in residence. Freedom was sweet, but the booze soon brought about her downfall – and Doreen's, too; and back they trooped to Wentworth. Doreen was imprisoned straight away, but Lizzie was at first released on bail; so, in order to be with her friend, Lizzie embarked on a mad shoplifting spree to get herself arrested.

Social worker Paul Reed set about trying to locate Lizzie's family, and two women who claimed to be her daughter and grand-daughter came forward. They were frauds, trying to get their hands on Lizzie's money to pay for surgery for the little girl. When Lizzie learnt the truth she pretended she'd known all the time. For a lonely old woman, two strangers who needed her were as good as real family.

NOELENE BOURKE, played by Jude Kuring, was unrelievedly corrupt, and determined to pass on her skills to her children. She failed with her eldest child, a gormless boy called Col who bungled a burglary and was shot dead in the ensuing police siege. Daughter Lianne (Tracey-Jo Riley) followed her mother into crime without prompting, and then young Wayne and Norelle were willing accomplices to their mother's villainy. Noelene's mother kept her hand in, too.

The most consistently unloved inmate of Wentworth, Noelene was always hatching some little scheme or other and delighted in her own criminal achievements. She would rather steal money than accept social security.

On the eve of her first release from Wentworth she smashed the recreation-room's new television set – though she was long gone when the deed was discovered. Enjoying her new liberty, she set about teaching daughter Lianne the finer points of burglary. She left the girl to keep watch while she took a crowbar to a factory door. Sadly, at the first sign of trouble the girl scarpered, and Noelene had to face the music alone. Soon back in Wentworth, Noelene was confronted by Bea, who had not been amused by the smashed telly. Bea walloped her, then told the mystified Noelene to parade her bloody nose before haemophobic Jim Fletcher!

Lianne soon visited Noelene to ask what she should do to support the Bourkes. Noelene advised burglary ('Gran'll tell you what to take, what'll sell'), but fortunately prison social worker Jean Vernon buttonholed Lianne, persuaded her to claim the dole and gave Lianne her address: Meg's flat, where she was staying. Lianne saw no reason to walk to the dole office, so she stole Jean Vernon's car.

At the dole office Lianne met a boy, and later his mate, but between them they still had no money and no great talent for crime. They bungled an attempt to steal *six hotdogs*, and then Lianne said, 'I know where we can lay our hands on some cash,' and took them off to Meg's flat. Meg knew who was responsible, but Jean Vernon persuaded her to do nothing about it. Noelene was unconcerned by the burglary but outraged by the news that a Bourke had claimed the dole. Jean Vernon even took Lianne home with her and recommended her for a job as a checkout girl at the local supermarket. Alas, she kept the job for only one day, was sacked and then went off with her boyfriend to rob a petrol station. It went wrong, and little Lianne soon joined her mother in gaol.

At liberty again, Noelene got a job as a tea-lady in an office-building, stealing money from handbags and jacket-pockets as she went on her rounds. During this time Lianne became involved in Judith Bryant's protests over the death of Sharon Gilmore and fell to her death from the prison roof. The police came to the office-building to break the news gently to Noelene, but their arrival coincided with the discovery that Noelene was a thief. All sympathy for her evaporated, and she was arrested.

Noelene believed that Bea Smith was responsible for Lianne's death, until Bryant explained what happened. Because Bryant felt guilty about Lianne's death, she became Noelene's protector. Anyone who wanted to hit Noelene would have to get past Bryant first; but since Bryant had a pacemaker no one dared fight her. All Noelene had to do was dodge behind Bryant at the first sign of trouble.

With only Gran to look after little Wayne and Norelle, Noelene was desperate for cash, fearing the kids would be taken into care. She plotted to steal bookie Margo's 'stash', but couldn't locate it.

Ironically, she did acquire a lot of money – and from Margo. One of her bets paid off!

Noelene's downfall came at the factory. She guessed that Kay White, the overseer, was helping herself to bolts of cloth, and asked for a piece of the action as the price of her silence. White agreed, arranged for Noelene to throw a bolt of cloth through a window to the waiting Wayne Bourke, then tipped off the boss, Andrew Reynolds. Wayne got away, but Vera ordered all the women back to Wentworth. Despite her protests, Noelene was accused of repeated thefts from the factory and was transferred to Barnhurst. Kay White went to Wentworth, and the truth about Noelene came out.

JUDITH BRYANT, played by Betty Bobbitt, was a Melbourne taxi-driver besotted with devious drug-dealer Sharon Gilmore. She contrived to get herself arrested in order to be with her sweetheart, who treated her like a doormat.

Bryant was American, and at school had had a lesbian affair with one of her teachers. When the truth came out the teacher lost her job and hanged herself, and Bryant's father threw his daughter out.

Bryant was found to have a heart condition and went to hospital to be fitted with a pacemaker.

Sharon Gilmore died, and Jock Mackay boasted to Bryant that he'd killed her. So when Davo merely suspended Mackay (who denied the charge to her) Bryant organised a prison protest that ended in a rooftop demo for the benefit of television cameras. It was during this demo that

Lianne Bourke fell off the roof to her death. Bryant felt responsible, and when Lianne's doting mother, Noelene, found herself back in Wentworth she took Noelene's side against the others and even aided her in some of her swifties.

When news came that Bryant's father was dying, she felt a pang of remorse – they'd been estranged for many years. But she was refused permission to go to see him in America. So she set her mind on escape. Hearing how Bea had once escaped from hospital after being stabbed in a brawl, Bryant managed to stand too close to the controls of the tumble-drier, short-circuit her pacemaker and collapse. Once in hospital, she lost no time in scarpering – clobbering a policewoman and stealing her uniform, and eventually

turning up at the home of Pauline, a former lover. Here she learnt that her father had already died. This left her with nothing more to do but try to get out of the country. She went to the Weasel, the notorious Melbourne forger, to arrange for a false passport. But before she could collect it and make good her escape her friend Pauline decided to dob her in.

DOREEN MAY ANDERSON BURNS, played by Colette Mann, was Wentworth's dopey dumpling. Davo alone recognised that Doreen was not a bad girl, just weak. Fletcher, on the other hand, was convinced Doreen was degenerate, having found her in bed with Lyn Warner. But Doreen's lesbianism seemed to have been 'prison issue': she had a baby when in her teens and was happily (if distantly) married to Kevin, and had never been as aggressively lesbian as Franky or Sharon.

Teddy-bear-clutching Doreen was initially one of Franky Doyle's crowd, and when Franky escaped she went with her. They were on the run for a couple of weeks, but then they were cornered, Franky was shot dead and Doreen was returned to Wentworth. Bitter and angry, Doreen tried to be a hard case, though this mostly seemed to consist of using her bulk to elbow weaker girls aside – especially 'Wonky' Warner. She pulled her hair back, found herself a couple of henchwomen, and for a few weeks made herself thoroughly objectionable. It didn't

Opposite Doreen Burns (Colette Mann) and Judith Bryant (Betty Bobbitt) brew their own grog

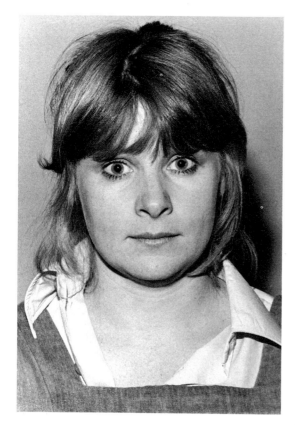

last, of course: Doreen was basically too nice.

Doreen was the principal victim of twisted psychologist Peter Clements when he came to Wentworth to do research. Given access to her file, he learnt of her lesbian associations and confronted her with them. Completely crushed, Doreen went into a catatonic trance, was taken off to a psychiatric hospital and was out of the series for some time.

She was eventually returned to Wentworth, and in time was released on parole into the care of the halfway house, where she was former inmate Karen Travers's first customer. She found a job at a local factory under an assumed name, and in the brief time that she worked there – before her true identity was discovered and she was sacked – she found true love with van-driver Kevin Burns (Ian Gilmour). He continued to be besotted even after he had learnt the truth about her background. In time they became engaged. Kevin had also been sacked, and was then a freelance van-driver.

While Doreen was at the halfway house her great friend Lizzie was also released, and the pair of them teamed up again. Kevin went along with Doreen's plan for Lizzie to come to live with them once they were married.

But true love had not allowed for Lizzie and the grog. On a bender one afternoon, she and Doreen ran out of both grog and money, so they decided to rob a grog-shop. Lizzie had one of her famous coronaries, but the robbery went wrong and both women were arrested. Doreen, who was on parole, was sent straight back to Wentworth, but Lizzie was simply released on bail. Unable to cope on her own, she went on a shoplifting spree to get herself arrested, and the police couldn't understand why she was so delighted when they obliged.

Doreen had been separated from her mother twenty years earlier, and had completely lost touch; but her mother (played by Anne Haddy), who was dying, came in search of her. There was a touching reunion, and when her mother did die shortly afterwards she left everything to Doreen, including a splendid house. Property developers had their eye on that street, and they managed to buy up a block of houses – but not Doreen's, which was bang in the middle of where they wished to build. A heavy was sent to the prison to put pressure on Doreen. The heavy found an ally in relief warder Jock Mackay, who agreed to persuade Doreen to sell in return for a generous payment. He contrived to get Doreen sent to solitary and visited her there. She was too frightened to talk, but Mackay was overheard on one occasion by Sharon Gilmore. She overplayed her hand, Mackay killed her, Vera saw him receiving money in the pub, and in the ensuing commotion at Wentworth all was revealed and Doreen kept her house.

Life was never simple for simple Doreen. Andrew Reynolds (a Melbournian Mike Baldwin) needed cheap labour at his clothing factory to complete a government contract, and Doreen became one of his workers. At the factory Vince Talbot the supervisor was much taken by Doreen, trapped her in the storeroom and threatened to accuse her of stealing if she didn't give herself to him. Doreen heard that the company's delivery contract was out to tender. She agreed to pleasure Vince if he would help Kevin, who was short of money, to secure the contract. He agreed, but Davo got to hear of her use of inside information, Kevin was deprived of the work, and all Doreen's sacrifices proved to have been in vain. Once again poor little Doreen had made a mess of everything.

Doreen discovered she was pregnant. All advised her to have an abortion – but in the mean time Bea was determined to exact revenge. Now, Kay White owed Vince money; she lured him to the prison under the pretext of paying him off, but ensured that he arrived during the women's exercise period – a lethargic attempt at volleyball. As he returned to the main gate, the women staged one of their famous diversions to hold Vera's attention while Bea, Doreen and Judith Bryant caught Vince and gave him a good kicking. Back in Davo's office, he thought it better to pretend that he had simply fallen over. But Kay White was aggrieved that her part in the scheme was not rewarded more generously by Bea and went to Davo to tell her the truth.

Doreen was one of the few characters in the entire series with whom one could really have any sympathy.

ROSALIND COULSON, played by Sigrid Thornton, was one of life's losers. The daughter of the woman murdered by Toni McNally, she lay in wait for McNally outside the court and shot her. Naturally she found herself inside Wentworth. As acting governor, Fletch put Roz in Bea's cell. Bea took the girl under her wing and, when Big Martha Eves tried to take revenge on Roz for murdering McNally, galloped to the rescue, flattening the Big M – gallantry which put Bea in solitary.

Roz had a touching faith in her own innocence, and fully expected the court to release her. After all, she reasoned, McNally murdered her mother and got away with it and she was simply doing the law's job. Roz was stunned when she returned to Wentworth after her trial to begin a life sentence. She was adamant that no prison was going to hold her for the rest of her life and began to plot her escape. She bungled one attempt to get out, but helped the terrorist Dominguez with her own escape-plan and when the guerrillas stormed the prison (staff having been given drugged coffee) they took her along. She changed her mind, however, when Davo, who had *not* drunk the coffee, confronted the gang and was shot in the arm.

After this, she apparently reconciled herself to a long stretch in Wentworth and began to study in the prison library.

ERICA DAVIDSON, played by Patsy King, was the woman who thought she ran Wentworth, and was constantly amazed to discover that she didn't. The prisoners did. Nicknamed 'Davo', she was a barrister, the daughter of an eminent judge and divorced, and always immaculately coiffed and dressed.

As a prison governor she was less than adequate, feebly suspending and then reinstating the women's privileges in an attempt to maintain control. Consequently she enjoyed an uneasy relationship with the Prison Department, and on one occasion came very close to being sacked. She knew that waiting behind her was Jim Fletcher, who had definite views on how the prison ought to be run, and behind *him* was Vera Bennett, who had long been after the top job. How much worse Wentworth would have been under either of these two was amply demonstrated when Davo resigned over the pressure being put on her to treat Toni McNally as

a special case. Within hours Jim Fletcher had alienated both prisoners and staff – much to the delight of Vera, who was convinced that she would take over when Fletch's administration finally collapsed. But Davo was persuaded to withdraw her resignation, Vera was thwarted, and Wentworth returned to the control of the prisoners.

In her time she was shot by guerrillas as she tried to prevent the escape of the freedom-fighter Dominguez (only prompt action by Rosalind Coulson in grabbing the gun-barrel prevented the shot from entering Davo's heart), held hostage by women in the prison (on account of her failure to perceive that the mysterious death of Sharon Gilmore might possibly demand serious attention), and kidnapped and threatened with having her fingers cut off.

She enjoyed a brief fling with Andrew Reynolds, owner of the small clothing firm at which the women were working on day-release. He was ardent but married, and Davo at first made it clear that she was quite prepared to eat and drink at his expense but he must put aside all thoughts of her returning any favours. But she finally dropped her objections.

This immediately proved embarrassing, because Vera Bennett had learnt of Reynolds's scheme to pay the women to work on garments not included in the government contract. She informed Davo (with ill-concealed delight) that her boyfriend was a crook. Davo was involved in a heated phone-call to Reynolds, saying that the only reason she was not withdrawing the women's labour completely

was that she knew how much the factory project meant to them.

They made things up, but when Kay White ran off with the payroll, and eventually turned up in Wentworth, Davo realised that all contact with Reynolds would have to cease. She withdrew the women from the work project, and even tried to lay the blame for it on them. Alas, the White caper made the papers, Vera saw it and – scenting the downfall of Davo – submitted a report to the Department. Before you could say 'loss of privileges', Ted Douglas was in Davo's office informing her that (a) she had been a fool and (b) there would have to be an inquiry.

Davo's immediate reaction was to rush round to Reynolds's factory to console him in his hour of trial. At a tender moment *Mrs* Reynolds turned up. Davo made her excuses and left, but it did not stop Mrs Reynolds from informing Andrew that she was going to seek a divorce.

Reynolds seemed to think that this changed everything, but Davo informed him that she was not prepared to sacrifice her career for love. Later Davo confessed all to Meg, having resolved never to see Reynolds again.

JANET DOMINGUEZ, played by Deirdre Rubenstein, was a political prisoner, briefly in Wentworth awaiting extradition. During her stay all the staff were on alert for a guerrilla raid to rescue her. Rosalind Coulson befriended her and agreed to help her with her escape-plan – if she could come, too. Dominguez agreed, and at the appropriate time Roz duly drugged the prison coffee. While the staff – with the exception of Davo – slept, the guerrillas (armed to the teeth) broke in, liberated Dominguez and Coulson, and made off. But they encountered Davo. One of them shot her in the arm, to Roz's horror. By this time the police had arrived, so their plans were frustrated.

TED DOUGLAS, played by Ian Smith, was the generally disliked, pen-pushing rule-fanatic who worked for the Department of Corrective Services. He left the Department and the series after he was filmed in the act of illegally accepting money. Later in the series, when Anne Reynolds (Gerda Nicholson) had taken over as the Wentworth governor, Erica Davidson took over from Ted Douglas as the visiting representative from the Department.

FRANKY DOYLE (née Frieda Joan Doyle), played by Carol Burns, was a sad and lonely illiterate lesbian. Until Sharon Gilmore arrived, she was the only aggressively lesbian character in the series. Doreen's tendencies were far more obliquely handled. Franky became besotted with Karen Travers – largely on account of Karen's education, of which the uneducated Franky was grudgingly jealous – but her love was not returned. Travers in fact made it quite clear how disgusting she found Franky's advances.

Loved by no one, the only ray of light in Franky's life was her younger brother, Gary (Greg Stroud). He visited her, and together they planned the little farm they

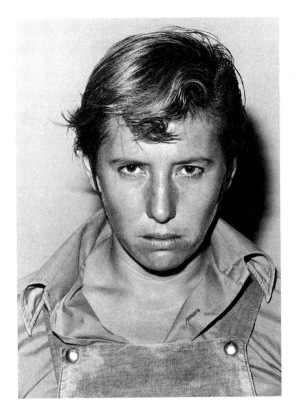

SUZI DRISCOLL, played by Jacqui Gordon, was the inmate who probably caused one of the biggest upsets at Wentworth. She tried to escape through the air-conditioning pipes but got stuck, jammed the system and sent the temperature inside soaring. Large ladies were melting all over the place. Suzi was let out, and stayed at the hostel run by Judith Bryant. There she conducted a mercy killing on another former inmate, Hazel Kent, who had a brain tumour. It landed Suzi back inside, but the hostel was named Driscoll House after her.

MARTHA EVES, played by Kate Jason, was slow-thinking and slow-talking. Martha – or 'The Big M' – was despised by everyone, but came in useful as hired muscle for those who felt they needed protection.

She was a minder for Toni McNally, wife of Melbourne's Mr Big, who, while on remand on a murder charge, usurped Bea's authority by supplying the women with illicit booze and funny cigarettes. Eventually Toni went for trial, was acquitted of murder, but was shot dead by her victim's daughter, Rosalind Coulson, outside the court. Roz quickly found herself in Wentworth. Martha naturally sought revenge for Toni's death, but Bea came to Roz's rescue, flattened Martha and took the girl under her wing.

Martha next befriended child-murderer Bella Albrecht, and kept her out of harm; but, ironically, when even Bella tired of her and called her a cretin Martha drowned her in a washbasin and was taken off to a more secure prison.

would have when she was finally released. Her brother was killed in a farm accident – a tractor overturned on top of him. Cruelly deprived of this dream, Franky went berserk, smashed up the recreation-room and threatened to throw herself off the roof.

Soon afterwards, Franky escaped with Doreen. They were on the run for several weeks – at one point dressed as nuns! – but were eventually cornered by the police. Franky was shot dead; and Doreen, recaptured, became temporarily bitter and vicious. Franky was the first in a long line of rivals for Bea Smith's authority and the only one for whom we felt any sympathy in defeat.

JOAN 'THE FREAK' FERGUSON, played by Maggie Kirkpatrick, arrived after Vera Bennett left. The Freak became as popular as Franky Doyle in the early days. This warder was supremely vindictive and a lesbian molester of the feebler prisoners. Unlike Vinegar Vera, she was truly corrupt and sexually rampant. Always behind the worst drugs-rackets and other inside fiddles, the nights were her best times. When the audience saw her wearing black gloves they knew she was about to conduct a 'body search' on an unsuspecting inmate, usually a new, young one.

During her reign of terror the storylines became more and more bizarre. A high spot was the fight between the Freak and Bea, who had vowed to kill her. Bea tried to strangle the Freak and hit her over the head with an iron bar. The Freak recovered strength enough to bang Bea's head on the ground and almost kill her. But later, when the Freak was about to be burnt to death in the fire she had Chrissie Latham start in the library, Bea saved her at the last minute. The Freak had planned the fire as part of her strategy to have the already reprimanded governor Anne Reynolds (Gerda Nicholson) sacked and to get the governor's job herself. An inmate called Mouse (Jentah Sobott) – so called because she was always quivering in fear – died in the fire.

MONICA FERGUSON, played by Lesley Baker, was the Gangster's Wife in Wentworth. A rather small gangster. 'Big Monnie' was kept at arm's length by Bea Smith. They did once have a fight, in the course of which Bea was stabbed, but they had a grudging respect for each other and were united in their contempt for Noelene Bourke.

Monnie's greatest misfortune was to be married to miserable little Fred (Gary Files), who had sought consolation with a bosomy tart called Blossom Crabtree (Linda Keane) while Monnie was away. It turned out that Blossom was only hanging around with Fred because of Monnie's loot, which was stashed away somewhere and which Fred was determined to get his hands on. In due course Monnie was paroled, and she returned home to reclaim her loot. Fred stole it and ran off with Blossom. Unfortunately for Fred, Blossom's boyfriend and accomplice, Bruce Starr, turned up, and he and Blossom stole Monnie's stolen money from Fred. Fred crawled back to Monnie, who beat him up in one of the most memorable scenes in the entire series. Assailed from all sides, Fred sought police protection. Monnie was arrested – as were Blossom and Bruce.

It so happened that deputy governor Fletcher was in need of money at the time, and when Crabtree found herself in Wentworth he made a deal with her. When the time came, he double-crossed her, returned the money to the authorities and pocketed the reward.

JIM FLETCHER, played by Gerard Maguire, was a former army sergeant who had volunteered for service in Vietnam, had later entered the prison service and eventually become deputy governor of Wentworth. Dour Jim was a male chauvinist who would appear to have been the natural ally of Vera Bennett, but even he found some of her more extreme attitudes disquieting.

Fletch was transferred from a men's prison, and made no secret of the fact that he regarded being deputy governor of a women's prison as definitely a bad career-move. He was horrified by lesbian relationships such as that between Doreen and Lyn Warner – although it was completely innocent. He also thumped Monica Ferguson soon after his arrival. Fletch was married to Leila (Penny Ramsay) with a couple of sons, but was separated at the time of entering the series. It turned out that his ideas about a woman's place (at the sink) caused the split. However, he and his wife got back together again soon after.

Fletch was dogged by his experiences in Vietnam, and would become momentarily immobilised if something caused him to recall those times. The problem turned out to be haemophobia, and when the women found out about it – it was leaked by twisted psychologist Peter Clements – they laid plans to exploit the situation. They organised a first-aid session, with fake blood. Jim went to pieces and was reprimanded by Davo. The women planned to follow up this success by organising a blood-donor session, but this came to nothing.

Fletch double-crossed the double-crossing Blossom Crabtree and claimed the reward for returning the stolen money. This helped to get him back in his wife's good books (she complained he didn't earn enough). But he fell prey to the charms of one of the inmates, and this brought nothing but trouble.

Fletch was fiercely loyal to his mates. One of these from Nam days, Geoff Butler (Ray Meagher), 'a bit of a character', turned up – he was actually trying to recruit Jim to his band of mercenaries – and they became very chummy again. Unknown to Jim, Geoff was a head case, given to bashing gays in pub toilets; and, to make matters even worse, he took a shine to Meg Jackson. Eventually the truth came out, the police were called to Meg's flat. Cornered, Geoff thumped Meg, but was captured by the cops.

When Davo resigned in protest at the pressure put upon her to go easy on Toni McNally, Jim stepped in as acting governor. He had always considered Davo too liberal in her approach, and a disastrous period followed in which Jim imposed so strict a regime that it alienated staff as well as prisoners and provoked a strike. Davo was brought back, and Jim was relegated to deputy once more.

Fletch's attitude softened when mother

and daughter Vivienne and Caroline Simpson were remanded to Wentworth on a charge of murdering Vivienne's brutish husband. Vivienne couldn't take prison life and was eventually released on bail (put up by Fletch through Paul Reed). After a while daughter Caroline also agreed to be bailed in the same fashion by Fletch, who was by this time thoroughly smitten. Although the rules strictly forbade it, Jim made secret visits to Caroline at the halfway house, and a cosy romance blossomed. Needless to say, wife Leila chucked Fletch out when she learnt of the affair, and he went to live in a dingy bedsitter where Caroline visited him for afternoons of passion.

In the mean time, Caroline's estranged husband resurfaced and objected to her affair with Jim. He chanced to meet Jim's pal Geoff Butler, who had received a suspended sentence and bore a grudge because Jim gave evidence at the trial. Between them they hatched a plot to get back at all concerned, though Caroline's husband didn't realise his new accomplice was mad and planned to kill his old buddy Fletch. The outcome was that Caroline's husband unwittingly delivered Geoff Butler's bomb to Fletch's apartment-block, Jim's wife and sons arrived on a surprise visit, collected the parcel from the lobby and took it up to his room. It exploded just outside his door, killing all three of them.

Fletch went on leave. A replacement, the vicious and corrupt Jock Mackay, arrived, enjoyed a brief romantic interlude with Vera, beat and blackmailed Doreen and killed Sharon Gilmore. Even Davo

had to accept that he had gone too far, and she suspended him. Fletch returned.

The chief problem in Fletch's life remained Vera. She was relieved of the deputy governorship because the Department felt that only a man could toughen up the staff. Davo's wishy-washy rule was deemed a disaster, and she was close to being relieved of her post. When Fletch applied for the job of governor of Barnhurst, Vera could scarcely conceal her delight.

AGNES FORSTER, played by Lois Ramsay, was Paul Reed's successor as Wentworth social worker. 'One year off retirement', Agnes was clearly based on the dotty old English spinster best typified by Margaret Rutherford's Miss Marple. She had a roomful of pot-plants, a cat called Butchy, a passion for tea-drinking and a habit of addressing everyone as 'dear' ('My name is Miss Bennett,' Vera corrected her firmly. 'Yes, dear,' came the reply).

Somewhat taken aback by Agnes's habit of drinking tea all day and leaving work early, while showing no interest in the women's files, Davo tartly suggested that she start doing some work. When she forgot to organise compassionate leave for Lizzie Birdsworth, Lizzie called her a lazy bitch and went berserk, scattering pot-plants and kitty litter all over her office. Later Vera discovered Agnes slumped across her desk; she raised the alarm, but Agnes was not dead – she had simply nodded off!

MARGO GAFFNEY, played by Jane Clifton, was the prison bookie. Her 'stash'

Margo Gaffney (Jane Clifton), rather the worse for wear, is supported by Chrissie Latham (Amanda Muggleton) and Bea Smith (Val Lehman)

was much coveted. Noelene, strapped for cash because her family were having a hard time, kept trying to get her hands on it – without success. Margo and Bea Smith were essentially soulmates, despite Margo's resentment when Bea attempted to control where and when Margo could take bets. Bea placed an embargo on bookmaking at the factory lest it compromise the work programme and interfere with her plan to deal with randy foreman Vince Talbot. Margo became Bea's accomplice in this scheme, and even pulled the switch when Bea rigged her machine to electrocute him. The betting embargo had unfortunately come too late to stop Margo from becoming locked in battle with factory overseer Kay White, who fancied herself as a backer of horses but did not do terribly well with her bets with Margo. For a while it looked as if these gambling debts might prove irrecoverable; but when Kay found herself in Wentworth she faced having to settle her debts – with bruises if not with money. Margo – working in the kitchen under the less than keen eye of kitchen supervisor Mrs O'Reagan – put detergent in Kay's food, but was prevented from drenching the next meal with Tabasco by the arrival Mrs Davidson. (Kay's complaint that the food tasted terrible met with no real response from either staff or inmates, who knew already.)

Margo did not have things all her own way: her first face-to-face confrontation with Kay ended with Kay punching her in the stomach. But Margo was not long in taking revenge. At the prison barbi she served Kay a hotdog with glass in it. Blood spouted from Kay's mouth.

SHARON GILMORE, played by Margot Knight, was Wentworth's lesbian drug-dealer. She had been delivering drugs to a party at which Paul Reed's son, Tony, was a guest when the police raided the joint. Tony was sent away for a few months, but Sharon received six years. A nasty piece of work, she tried to worm her way into Doreen's affections by reviving the poor girl's lesbian tendencies. She enjoyed brief popularity by arranging to have exotic substances smuggled in by her doting lover Judith Bryant. Bryant was so distraught at being separated from her beloved that she arranged to have herself caught smuggling and was herself imprisoned. Once Bryant was inside, however, Sharon played fast and loose with her affections.

Sadistic warder Jock Mackay eventually bumped Sharon off. Sharon had overheard him threaten and then assault Doreen, so she tried to blackmail him. He threw her down some stairs to shut her up.

MEG JACKSON, played by Elspeth Ballantyne, is the Mrs Nice of Wentworth. The reason she is caring and humane with the women is that she was the daughter of a crim and was actually born in prison. Her husband, Bill (Don Barker), was the social worker at Wentworth, but was stabbed to death by Chrissie Latham during a prison riot early in the series, leaving Meg a widow with a teenaged son called Marty. Meg subsequently tried to find a fresh love-interest – first with Dr Greg Miller and then with Geoff Butler, Fletch's nutty Nam pal who beat her up. She eventually married Bob Morris (Anthony Hawkins).

Meg's caring nature threw her together with the social workers: first, she befriended Jean Vernon, who came to share her flat and misguidedly invited larcenous Lianne Bourke to stay there, too; and, second, she warmed to Paul Reed, who was out of step with the other members of staff and enjoyed an uneasy relationship with Davo. Meg took a motherly interest in his troublesome son, Tony. She was constantly at odds with Vera and was not afraid to stand up to Davo when she thought she was being unreasonable. Relations with Davo were rather difficult when the governor believed that Meg and Paul were plotting to undermine her authority by taking an interest in the women's welfare.

Not surprisingly, Meg was seen as a pushover by the women – though, to their credit, they respected her compassion and didn't try to exploit it. But when Lizzie was required to have a tactical 'coronary' Meg was the one person before whom she had to be sure to have it. Vera and Fletch would simply have walked away.

When tarty Chrissie Latham, who'd stabbed Meg's husband, returned to Wentworth to complete her sentence, Meg was not pleased. But she coped. The other prisoners seemed more concerned by this crass departmental decision than the other members of staff.

Determined to make a fresh start in her life, she moved to a new flat. Before very long she was taking an interest in the next-door neighbours, whose nocturnal rumpuses were keeping her awake. The husband was a drunken bum, and the wife, Gail Summers, inadequate and oppressed. Meg noticed bruises on one of the children's arms, and soon felt obliged to call in the authorities, believing that the husband was walloping the kids. In fact it was the *wife* who was doing the walloping, and soon she found herself in Wentworth. Meg felt guilty at having reported the wretched creature – the act which put her behind bars and exposed her to the anger of the other prisoners – and took a deep interest in her, aided by Paul Reed and Captain Barton of the Salvation Army. Happily, Gail got off with a two-year suspended sentence, which eased Meg's conscience considerably. (Meg was later to experience life on the other side for herself when she was convicted of perjury.)

When the women rioted to protest at the Sharon Gilmore murder cover-up, Meg was held hostage (with a garden fork held to her throat).

CHRISSIE LATHAM, played by Amanda Muggleton, was an unappetising cockney tart, unloved by anyone. She was removed from Wentworth early in the series after she had stabbed Meg Jackson's husband to death with a pair of scissors during a prison riot. Eddie the Electrician identified her as the culprit.

After a while she was returned to Wentworth, with scant regard for Meg's feelings. She was by then pregnant – though the precise sequence of events was unclear. It appeared that she had been offering herself to male inmates and members of staff of the adjacent men's prison – at one point it was suggested that even the governor might be the father – and in time, after a difficult premature labour following a prison brawl, she

brought forth a scrawny child, considered unlikely to live. But all turned out well. Chrissie became a doting mum, and was last seen in the maternity wing.

TONI MCNALLY, played by Pat Bishop, was the wife of the Godfather of the Melbourne underworld. She shot the woman who had been having an affair with her husband. On remand she took over the prison during one of Bea's regular trips to the pound, and kept the women sweet with smuggled booze and funny cigarettes. Martha Eves was her bodyguard. Her husband clearly had influence in the higher reaches of the prison service, because pressure was brought to bear on Davo to go easy on McNally. Frustrated beyond endurance, Davo tendered her resignation.

In time McNally had her day in court and was acquitted – well, her husband had bought off all the witnesses – but as she left the court she was shot dead by Rosalind Coulson, daughter of the woman McNally had murdered.

MARILYN MASON, played by Margaret Laurence, was the pretty whore who is chiefly memorable for her long-running affair with Eddie the Electrician. He had been given the run of Wentworth in order to rewire it, found Marilyn and then found excuses to prolong his presence. They were lucky enough to discover a quiet corner of the prison roof in which to consumate their union, and eventually,

Opposite Chrissie Latham (Amanda Muggleton) helping the police with their enquiries

touchingly, Eddie proposed. But their antics were discovered by the authorities, the electrical firm lost the contract and Eddie was sacked.

On her release, Marilyn set up home in a dreary bedsit with Eddie. She struggled to find honest employment; but, demoralised by her failure, turned once more to her ponce, who returned her to her old ways. She broke Eddie's heart and ended up in Wentworth again. This time she was given a hard time by motherly Bea, who was disgusted at the way in which she had thrown away her chance of happiness.

DR GREG MILLER, played by Barry Quinn, was the Wentworth doctor until the wider world of medicine called him. The women regularly helped themselves to drugs and surgical alcohol while his back was turned. He eventually bought a run-down practice in a deprived area from an old doctor, but later settled into a country practice – though he did pop into Wentworth to tell the pre-pacemaker Judith Bryant that the chances of her dying on the operating-table were not really so great.

His later career was rather complicated. One of the Wentworth inmates, Pat O'Connell, who was eventually paroled, had a criminal son, David – among whose friends was a car thief called Shayne (Stefan Dennis) – who escaped from prison. To help her Greg rushed off to the house to warn them that the police were about to raid it. He turned up at the same time as the cops, and the bad guys assumed that he had tipped them off.

They determined to seek revenge. One night they crept up to Greg's downtown surgery, waited until his head was silhouetted in the lighted window and shot him – or thought they had. In truth they had missed the Doc completely and hit Karen Travers, with whom Greg was involved at the time. Brain surgery followed, then convalescence, and eventually Greg and Karen married.

'MUM', played by Mary Ward, was imprisoned for helping to speed the death of her sick husband. She was everyone's 'mum', offering sound common sense when it was needed. The garden was regarded as her special domain; and those who remembered her couldn't plant a bulb without fond memories flooding to mind.

She was released on parole, but her nice middle-class family were embarrassed by her and she moved into a seedy bedsit. She couldn't cope with life on the outside and contrived to get herself arrested again. However, once she was back inside she was visited by her grand-daughter, and when 'Mum' was released again the two of them set up home together. The girl became pregnant, and the strain of coping with all this, together with having to shelter Bea when she was on the run *and* have Karen Travers back in her life, eventually told. 'Mum' collapsed and died.

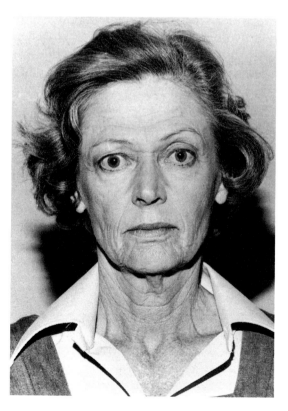

PAT O'CONNELL, played by Monica Maughan, was one of a family of misfits who landed in prison through inadequacy. Pat's son, David, who was in the neighbouring men's prison, was being beaten by the warders. He couldn't take any more and escaped. His mother was on parole at the time, and Dr Miller feared she would be implicated and returned to prison because of the escape. He rushed round to the house to warn her, but it was too late. Thus the train of events that led to Karen being shot in the head was innocently started. Pat was a decent sort, much liked by Bea.

KEN PEARCE, played by Tom Oliver, was a reformed hard man. After having served a long sentence for a violent crime he discovered the therapeutic power of Dramatic Art and set up a prisoners' drama organisation, touring prisons and encouraging prisoners to act out their frustrations, resentments and so on.

Paul Reed persuaded Davo to encourage Ken's efforts, but no one reckoned on hard man Pearce taking a shine to hard woman Bea Smith. To cut a long story short, one day, while the women were engaged in cultural pursuits, Ken and Bea retired to the recreation-room broom-cupboard. They were only *talking*, of course; but Sharon Gilmore betrayed them, the pair were hauled out of their love-nest, and Pearce was sent packing.

At one point Pearce's daughter fell in with a fast set and showed signs of going off the rails, so he arranged for her to spend twenty-four hours in Wentworth to make her realise what lay in store for her if she persisted on her wayward course. Bea did her Concerned Parent act, and impressed upon the girl that life behind bars was not fun.

PAUL REED, played by George Mallaby, was the Wentworth social worker, succeeding Jean Vernon (Christine Amor). He single-handedly brought up a son, Tony, who was something of a trial to his father. Tony became involved with a bad crowd, and was eventually imprisoned on drugs charges. Paul Reed and Meg Jackson were soulmates, frequently united in their compassion against the hanging-is-too-good-for-these-women attitude of Vera Bennett and Jim Fletcher. Davo once reacted sarcastically against Paul and Meg's chumminess, believing, as she always did, that they were seeking to undermine her authority.

Reed decided to go into partnership with his son in a car-repair workshop, and went off to Adelaide without letting anyone know. Captain Barton of the Salvation Army sat in for him for a while – but when Paul finally sent in his resignation from Adelaide a successor was appointed: Agnes Forster.

ANDREW REYNOLDS, played by John Lee, was Wentworth's answer to Mike Baldwin. He owned a clothing factory which landed an Important Government Contract, and if he failed to meet the deadline the company would go under. To avoid this Reynolds approached the Prison Department for some cheap labour, and Wentworth duly obliged. Only a limited number of places were available on the 'work programme', so competition among the women was fierce and the pressure on the lucky women to behave themselves was considerable.

Reynolds seemed quite unaware that he was sitting on top of a small mound of corruption. His supervisor, Vince Talbot, had taken a shine to Doreen. He blackmailed her into obliging him in the store-room. Bea found out about it and planned revenge. The first stage was to electrocute him by rigging one of the sewing machines; later she led an attack on him in the prison grounds.

The work programme – and Reynolds's future livelihood – were jeopardised when Noelene Bourke pushed her luck too far. She guessed that Kay White, Reynolds's assistant, was stealing bolts of cloth from the factory and asked for a piece of the action as the price of her silence. White agreed, then betrayed her; and the out-come was that Vera Bennett ordered all the women back to the prison. There were hasty phone-calls between the factory and Wentworth, and the work programme was saved.

Davo's judgement was no doubt clouded by the fact that she was being wined and dined by Reynolds. Reynolds asked the women to do unauthorised work (for ten dollars a week) on garments that were not part of the government contract. The union representative, Hazel Crow, discovered what was going on, protested to Vera and threatened a strike. Armed with this information – and heartened by the promise of a strike that could only serve to kill off the work programme – Vera confronted Davo with the news that her boyfriend was a crook.

Strong words were exchanged between Davo and Reynolds, but the project was allowed to continue because Davo knew how much it meant to the women. Reynolds then discovered that his assistant, Kay White, had scarpered with the payroll. It transpired that she was a compulsive gambler, and had 'borrowed' the payroll to back a horse. The horse actually won, and Kay returned to the factory with her winnings, intending to put the money back into the safe. But she did not know that her 'borrowing' had been discovered, and she was arrested. She protested that, as a compulsive gambler, she should be treated as a psychiatric case and not as a criminal. But it was all too late for Reynolds: his company was falling apart, Davo had finally rejected him, and his wife – returning suddenly to find Davo too close to Andrew for comfort and the company in ruins – had decided to divorce him.

BEATRICE ('BEA') ALICE SMITH, played by Val Lehman, was the Mrs Big (in every sense) of Wentworth. Big in size, voice and brainpower. There were occasional challenges to her authority – anyone who could offer the women booze and funny cigarettes smuggled in from outside could usually lure their allegiance away from Bea for a little while, especially when she was paying one of her regular visits to the pound. But, strictly speaking, Queen Bea ran the place, and did so from the beginning of the series. Paul Reed grasped very quickly that if he wanted to get any scheme working in the prison he had to sell it to Bea first.

Bea's greatest asset was her patience. She was prepared to bide her time, find exactly the right moment at which to strike, and then act fast and hard. The others were frequently bewildered by Bea's *apparent* indifference when someone was attempting to usurp her authority or acting in such a way as to risk making life hell for everyone. But Bea's willingness to wait and watch always paid off.

Bea was inside for double murder: she killed her husband's mistress and (as soon as she was released on parole) she killed her husband, who had, she felt neglected their daughter and was therefor responsible for the youngster's dalliance with drugs. But Bea had her hair done and

Opposite Bea Smith (Val Lehman) as defiant as ever. Gentle 'Mum' (Mary Ward) can only watch

bought new clothes first. Because of this background, everyone knew that *kids* and *drugs* were likely always to arouse an immediate and deep response from Bea. She was ruthless with drug-pushers in Wentworth, befriended imprisoned mums, and was foremost in the persecution of child-beater Gail Summers (though she softened after Gail's impassioned speech on the sheer hell of being a mum).

Her motherly instincts were never far below the surface: she was ever ready to protect the weak against the bully – and exacted revenge for factory supervisor Vince Talbot's rape of Doreen by electrocuting him at the factory and then leading an assault on him in the prison grounds (for which all the women lost a week's remission).

Life in Wentworth consisted largely of trials of strength between Davo and Bea. Even when Bea was sent to the pound and (in theory) cut off from all contact with the rest of the prison she managed to control the women. Meg Jackson, like Paul Reed, believed in collaborating with Bea to keep the women in line; Vera and Fletch saw her as the root of all evil and never missed an opportunity to put her in solitary. At the factory Reynolds annoyed Meg and Vera by calling Bea 'the boss' and treating her as such.

Bea was once involved in a fight with Monica Ferguson, in the course of which she was stabbed. Once in hospital, she lost no time in escaping, and had fun for a few weeks before being recaptured. (The police were eventually told of her whereabouts by the girl next door – played by Val Lehman's daughter – who resented Bea's attempts to mother her.)

Bea also discovered true love in the shape of Ken Pearce. Paul Reed sold her the idea of drama classes, about which she became very enthusiastic once she had met the organiser. (Previous schemes, for a prison newspaper and the manufacture of fluffy toys, had not fared well.) Soon romance was in the air, and the other women were obliged to improvise plays and wade through *A Midsummer Night's Dream* simply to provide scope for love to blossom. In the course of this strange affair Bea put Ken's wayward daughter on the straight and narrow for him. Of course, this affair could not last; one day Bea and Ken used the women's cultural efforts – on this occasion an art class by Kerry Vincent – as a diversion while they sneaked into the recreation-room broomcupboard for some stolen intimate moments. Sharon Gilmore betrayed them, and Ken was banished from the prison for ever.

GAIL SUMMERS, played by Susanne Howarth, was the pathetic mother driven to child abuse. Meg Jackson moved next door to the Summers family and soon discovered that the husband was a drunken bum and the wife, Gail, clearly inadequate, unable to keep the home tidy and look after her kids. The frequent rows kept Meg awake on many a night, until she eventually decided to investigate. She spotted bruises on one of the children, and concluded that his father was beating him. She notified the authorities, who arrived at the Summerses' flat to confront the brute of a father – only to discover the kid was being beaten by his *mother*. Gail was arrested and remanded to Wentworth.

At the prison, in view of the sensitive nature of the offence and the fact that crims take a very dim view of child-abusers, Davo decided that the truth should be kept quiet. She had not reckoned on miserable childless Vera, who took the earliest opportunity to let the women know precisely what Gail had done. They began to persecute her - though a long and heartfelt speech on the misery of motherhood did soften them somewhat. Jim Fletcher, whose own children were killed in an explosion, was not very sympathetic; but Meg, having caused the woman to be arrested in the first place, worked off her guilt by being very solicitous for the girl's welfare. When Gail was given a two-year suspended sentence, Meg could scarcely conceal her relief.

KAREN TRAVERS, played by Peita Toppano, was the well-educated, caring, decent, intelligent woman who really ought to have been governor. Unfortunately, she was a prisoner. Her sophistication (compared with the others) and her readiness to stand up for herself made for an uneasy relationship with Davo; while Vera deeply resented the privileges accorded to Karen simply because she could read and write, and gloated whenever Karen's plans were thwarted.

Karen became the object of Franky Doyle's affections, but was repelled by the very idea of lesbian passion.

In time Karen was permitted to attend university on a day-release scheme – though this privilege was suspended at the slightest hint of trouble inside the prison. At 'uni' she had to lie about her background, and things became rather tricky whenever any of her fellow-students suggested that they might go back to her place.

Her tutor at 'uni' was twisted psychologist Peter Clements (Carrillo Gantner). He knew all about her background, and this gave him the idea of applying for permission to conduct research within Wentworth – with disastrous results.

Eventually Karen was released on parole, and at first went to stay with an aunt. In time she was taken up by a civil rights activist who was a notorious lesbian. One of this woman's pet projects was a halfway house in which women released from prison could adjust to life in the outside world. She recruited Karen to help her. Karen moved into her house as her secretary. When a property became available, Karen moved in as warden: her first charge was Doreen.

It was during this time that she renewed her friendship with Greg Miller. (They had been romantically attached before Karen actually went to prison, and when they were both in Wentworth they were very chummy.) Greg had also kept in touch with 'Mum', who at that time was sharing a flat with her very pregnant grand-daughter. As the girl's time approached, Greg persuaded Karen to move in and take some of the strain off 'Mum'.

As his relationship with Karen deepened, Greg left the prison service and bought a run-down practice in a deprived area; but he was persuaded to make occasional calls at the prison. He became caught up in the troubles of Pat O'Connell, whose son was on the run. In attempting to protect Pat he innocently initiated the train of events which led to Karen being shot in the head instead of him. She pulled through and he married her.

KERRY VINCENT, played by Penny Downie, was transferred to Wentworth with special privileges on account of her remarkable artistic talent, after staff and prisoners had been introduced to the delights of culture by Ken Pearce. In fact Kerry Vincent was a mediocrity, but an unscrupulous agent had spotted an opportunity to do himself a lot of good. In time Kerry discovered the truth about the agent, hit him with an ashtray and then tried to kill herself.

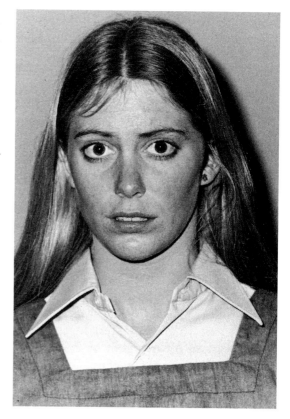

One comic sidelight: Vera, grudgingly acknowledging the girl's talent, informed Kerry that she had herself been a bit of an artist in her youth, and Kerry presented her with one of her own works. This canvas was eventually used as part of Davo's 'sting' to teach the agent a lesson. Desperate to acquire all Kerry's work, he paid an inflated price for it.

LYN WARNER, played by Kerry Armstrong, was disaster-prone. She drifted from one catastrophe to another, but she did not gain our sympathy in the way that Doreen did.

A country girl, she was the first Wentworth woman to obtain work outside the prison: she went to work at a local market-garden, but the boss's son took a shine to her, the father disapproved, and the whole scheme collapsed.

Her farmer father gradually rebuilt his relationship with her, and in time she was released to return to the family home. She was not out for long.

When Doreen returned to prison after her time on the run, bitter about the death of Franky, she decided to try to be a hard case. The only woman in the prison she could really terrorise was Lyn Warner, whom she called 'The Wonk' because . . .

well, Lyn Warner was *odd*. This couldn't last, of course: Doreen was essentially too good-natured to keep up this act. On the eve of Warner's release, she slept with Doreen, who was feeling very lonely. Next morning they were found in bed by Fletch, who clearly believed he had uncovered a mass of human degradation. In fact it was completely innocent.

Lyn set up home with a crim from the neighbouring men's prison. The boyfriend and his mate planned a wages-snatch, and when the driver cried off at the last minute the boyfriend persuaded Lyn – who was well advanced in pregnancy – to drive the getaway car. Everything went wrong, and Lyn found herself back in prison.

ANNE YATES, played by Kirsty Child, was a Wentworth warder who went bad and was sacked. Vera later met up with her again and, at a party in Yates's flat, met her business associate, George Lucas, and thought she had at last found true love. Unfortunately, the business was drug-trafficking, but Vera didn't discover this until it was almost too late. The whole racket fell apart, Yates was arrested, and Vera was deserted by her new boyfriend, who left her tied and gagged in her flat.

Now back at Wentworth as a prisoner, Yates was despised by the other women and one day, in an attempt to escape from them, she hid in a giant tumble-drier, accidentally locked herself in and suffocated.

3
ON THE OUTSIDE

COLETTE MANN is one of the few *Prisoner* actresses who'd really been to gaol – to teach and coach inmates in drama. Fair-haired, far slimmer, infinitely more intelligent and lower-voiced than her squeaking, teddy-bear-clutching character Doreen, Colette used to visit Pentridge prison in Melbourne to help men in A Division with movement, dance and acting instruction. Her career had started in 1971 with a role in *Godspell* and she has varied her work to include singing, dancing, choreography, radio braodcasting and campaigning for charities helping child victims of abuse. She is married to a freelance cameraman, and they have a two-year-old son Sam and expect a second child this year.

Colette, a law graduate, recalls the excitement in the 'business' when news about the planned series, *Prisoner*, came out in March 1978. 'Casting didn't start until the following October, but word had spread. There were about twelve women's roles and two men's – it's usually the other way around. Every actress in Australia was auditioning for it; there was quite a buzz, because it was obviously going to be a benchmark series. Women had never played strong roles before, roles which said: "I'm me, on my own." We'd always been someone's wife or girlfriend.

'I was well known for stage and musicals in those days, and it was a bit of a jump to go to television. I was approached first to play Lyn Warner or Marilyn, the prostitute.

'I read the scripts and asked to test for Doreen instead because she seemed safe and I really wanted to play scenes with Sheila Florance, who was a highly respected actress. In the end I tested with Val Lehman and got the part. We made eight episodes before it went out. I thought Doreen was very low key, but as soon as people started watching, Doreen and Lizzie were the dills of the piece and we began getting fan mail – far more than any of the other people in the cast. I liked old Doreen; she grew on me and grew up in her years there. She'd been raped, shot at; she'd escaped, got herself a boyfriend, married him, divorced, got another boyfriend and was a lesbian at other times depending on how the writers felt about

Picture page 64 Sheila Florance enjoying the sights on her way to a civic reception in Derby

it. Oh, and I also remember trying to hang myself in the laundry over an abortion. The focus shifted quite a bit over the years; we had several different producers – it was inevitable. Doreen even lost the teddy bear she used to clutch. As far as I recall, Noelene pulled its head off and then it was left in a tunnel. Lizzie and Doreen were in a tunnel for days after it collapsed. In reality we would have died but the viewers suspended their disbelief.

'I left after about four hundred episodes because I felt Doreen was repeating herself and it was hard-going. There was a feeling of camaraderie among the cast; you get to know people pretty well when you work that closely for so long.

'To relieve some of the strain I used to sing in a trio with two of the other actresses, Jane Clifton and Betty Bobbitt. We used to dress up to look very sophisticated in black sequins and we'd be introduced as inmates of Wentworth but we wouldn't do *Prisoner* jokes. We sang in clubs in Sydney on and off for about two and a half years. And in one of my breaks – "when Doreen was sent to The Third Floor" – that was always the sign the actress wanted time off to do a play or something – I did a film, *Kitty and the Bagman* with two other *Prisoner* people, Val Lehman and Gerald Maguire.'

Although Colette, now 40, has done so many different things since leaving the series, including commentating on sports events and a two-year stint in a comedy show, she is still remembered for Doreen by people in the street.

Colette is, however, grateful to her British fans. 'Three of Doreen's goofs have been shown a couple of times on *It'll Be Alright on the Night*,' she said. 'So far they have earned me a thousand dollars.'

SHEILA FLORANCE couldn't get her teeth into the role of Lizzie Birdsworth at first. The producers had asked her to take them out at the audition. The actress, who had 45 years' of experience behind her, didn't mess around. Anyway, she's a self-confessed exhibitionist. She slipped her dentures out and got the job. Soon it was impossible to think of anyone but little Sheila as raspy-voiced, leathery old Lizzie, Wentworth's oldest inmate. But the two women couldn't sound more different. Sheila has a cultured voice with little trace of her St Kilda, Melbourne, birth. Her mother was a dentist, her father a teacher, and she recalls she would be 'thumped' if she spoke 'Ocker'.

She began acting in Australia at the age of 16 but in 1935, aged 19, she came to England and appeared in many West End plays. She also travelled, and recalls a trip to the 1936 Olympics in Berlin where she happened to sit a few rows behind Adolf Hitler. Married and the mother of two young sons and pregnant with a third, she received news that her husband serving in France had been killed in the 1944 Normandy landings. That tragedy was followed by another – the devastating death of the new child, a girl aged only 10 months, dragged from her arms by the force of a bomb. Sheila had travelled to Bristol to join the Old Vic, and when she stepped off the train at Templemeads station. 'A bomb dropped near me, and my little girl was blown from my arms and

killed,' she told a Melbourne newspaper in 1979. Again she coped, threw herself into work with repertory companies and acted with such stars as Robert Donat, Emlyn Williams and Sid James. One night, appearing in *The Lisbon Story*, a play about espionage, in the West End, the air-raid sirens began. The cast and audience ran to the safety of cellars and Underground stations. Sheila was within 50 metres of the Underground when a shell exploded behind her. She was flung to the ground, thought herself dead but incredibly escaped with only cuts and bruises and, since the theatre was still standing, went on with the show the next night. She often said it was a good grounding for her profession. It certainly put the violent eruptions at Wentworth in perspective. Eventually she met a Polish fighter-pilot who'd seen her with friends in a pub and nagged them for her phone number. 'I was too unhappy at the time to bother much about him, but he kept calling and eventually I gave in and went out with him.'

There were more shocks as Jan was shot down three times, suffering severe injuries. But they were finally married in a spectacular ceremony at Nottingham Roman Catholic Church, although Jan had to walk down the aisle on crutches and was never completely well. With him, Sheila returned to Australia and had a child, but bad luck struck again and the girl died at the age of 18. Again there was her work in the theatre to help. A favourite role in 1962 was Lady Macbeth. Taking it fulfilled an ambition she'd had since the schoolgirl Sheila saw Dame Sybil Thorndike in the role.

For *The Shadow of Heroes* and *The Mating Season* she received two Melbourne Critics' awards. She appeared in the early soap *Bellbird*, in which she was 'killed off' five times, and did many radio plays. But it was only with the role of Lizzie Birdsworth – 'a lovable old rascal', as Sheila called her – in *Prisoner* that the recognition began. She was tickled pink that after forty-five years' work as an actress she was being stopped in the street and children would dance around her. In America 'I Love Lizzie' T-shirts went on sale as the series became a cult. 'When I watch Lizzie I see nothing of myself,' she said, 'but she makes me laugh.'

She took time out in 1980 to film a part in *Mad Max* with Mel Gibson. But chasing a bikie with a double-barrelled shotgun she fell into a hole and broke a leg. But she couldn't afford to play the invalid because by then her family had expanded. As well as three grandchildren she was bringing up a young boy who was a musical prodigy.

She left *Prisoner* in 1983 after 418 episodes. In the last few years life has again been hard. Jan died and Sheila herself has suffered from but beaten cancer. Determined never to retire, she looks back fondly on her Wentworth sentence. The performance won her several awards; but the real bonus, she says, was her lasting friendship with other 'inmates', notably Colette Mann and Val Lehman, alias Doreen and Bea.

CAROL BURNS spent four months playing Franky Doyle and never dreamt Wentworth's most tragic lesbian crim would be hailed as a 'sort of milestone' and haunt her for years to come. On balance she's pleased that the inmate they expected to become the most hated character on television is remembered with sympathy and even a smile. Franky didn't make Carol a big star, partly because Carol wasn't that interested in fame on television and also because she is almost unrecognisable from the spiky-haired, nicotine-stained bikie in dungarees who had a naked woman tattooed on her breasts.

Franky's voice came to Carol as she travelled on a train from Cairns soon after accepting the role. 'I listened to two little boys squabbling and one kept saying "piss orf" aggressively but with no real nastiness, and I copied that. The hairdo was the nearest I could get to Elvis Presley – I imagined Franky would have

him as a hero.' The mannish swagger as she walked was easy. The nicotine was from yellow food-colouring painted on her fingers, and Carol was shown how to roll a cigarette like she'd been doing it since she was ten. As she started playing the part she felt sad for the girl. 'She's a lost soul in a society where the bikie and the lesbian are misfits. I find a particular pathos in the fact that Franky has never had anyone to love or love her. She loves Karen because she represents something gentle and pure – something Franky can

never be.' Carol left the series after only a few months. She had asked to be written out, and the first plan was to have her commit suicide by jumping off the prison roof, but the final version had her being shot while on the run. Carol left because she objected to the decision to produce and screen two episodes a week. She did not think the quality of the scripts or the acting could be maintained, and many others shared her fears. 'Franky was a splendid, energetic character. I tried to bring out the vulnerability in her which I felt went with her youth. The lesbianism was almost incidental. They're just human beings, after all. I hoped social workers could use her in discussions because the series had such a wide appeal. I know it was watched by all sorts of people from a solicitor I knew to the lady in the launderette.

'I didn't tire of Franky, but I wanted her to go out with a bang and at the right time. Often producers try to over-extend the viable life of a character. The situations can become absurd, and we had a little of that with the women dressing up as nuns on one occasion. But Franky died rather well, and I was interested to see that she was referred to in the scripts for the next three years. I was in Los Angeles the night they showed her dying, and there was a huge wake and a parade down the street. We celebrated her death in a gay club.'

Before *Prisoner*, Brisbane-born Carol had worked in the theatre and had lectured in drama at a college of advanced education in Queensland. 'I always believed actors should be international people and I always liked to move on, to travel. I'd done about ten years in the theatre and had taken roles in a few miniseries and films and I thought it was time I tried a part in a commercial soap, since they form such a large part of my country's entertainment industry. And it has been fun to find *Prisoner* surfacing all over the world.'

Since Wentworth, Carol has appeared in several films, notably *Bad Blood* with Jack Thompson, starred in the television film *Eureka Stockade* and played Anastasia Hayes in *Strikebound*. 'I love playing women who stand up for their rights, perhaps because I'm not brave enough in my own life – I'm a middle-class coward,' she laughed. She has visited Britain many times, and settled in London with her composer husband Alan Lawrence three years ago. 'I had reached a height in my career in Australia but I had to start again from square one here. I turned down the offer of playing Franky in the *Prisoner: Cell Block H* stageplay. I didn't want to go back. I'm determined to do work of quality now, even if that means rather too much free time digging my vegetables in the garden or listening to Radio Four.'

ELSPETH BALLANTYNE is the sort of woman who 'shrivels at the merest hint of violence', who practically passes out with shock when a drunk swears in the street and who hates wearing any kind of uniform. Yet the timid Adelaide-born actress not only volunteered for what was probably Australia's most chaotic gaol with some of the most violent characters ever imagined; she was also one of the few to do the full stretch, staying till it ended seven years later. Her television life of crime and punishment as warder Meg Jackson may have been completely against her nature but, she said, it fitted in well with her home life at the time. It was a regular and well-paid 'day job', one which enabled her to bring up her schoolboy sons Matthew and Toby following her divorce from actor Denis Miller. She also liked Meg, although she never let her sons watch her in the show. It wasn't suitable, she said.

Coming from a theatrical family – her mother was an actress, her father a director – she'd made her stage début in *Macbeth* aged eight but decided to train for a 'proper job' as a lab technician before taking the plunge, winning a top scholarship for drama school. After several years in the theatre, she'd starred in many popular Australian television series and was well-known as the butter-wouldn't-melt Lori Chandler in Australia's *Bellbird* which was a television country story similar to 'The Archers'. Meg was also a 'goodie', but tough, too.

'I saw her as a warm compassionate mediator between the governor and the prisoners,' she told me, 'somebody who because of her attitude would arouse the ire of Vera Bennett. Vera's outlook was that the prisoners were animals, while Meg thought there was hope for everyone.' Elspeth had been to a couple of real Melbourne prisons: to Pentridge men's prison, as part of the cast of prisoner Jim McNeil's play about prison life *How Is*

Your Garden Growing? to entertain the inmates; and to Fairlea for some research for her role.

'But what I actually enjoyed most were the laughs. There was always someone in the show who was really dotty. There were many great comics among the actresses – Sheila and Colette were very funny people. I was always giggling in my scenes with Fiona Spence, who played Vera. Once it took me about twelve times to get through a brief conversation with her. The director was sick of me – he threatened that if I didn't pull myself together he'd punish me by making me do the scene after everything else at the end of the day. And it may sound silly but it was always a great relief when one of the inmates got over the wall or hid something from the warders.'

Meg had her difficult moments, of course. She was robbed, gang-raped, shot, beaten, held at knife- and fork- point. She lost a husband and had another prospective husband change his mind about marrying her after having his kneecaps shot off.

'She was blown up in a brick factory with Erica, the governor, once,' said Elspeth chuckling. 'In reality we would now be in tiny fragments but Meg suffered a damaged spleen and Erica a broken arm, I think.' And at one stage she had to be poisoned and then given an antidote by some of the prisoners. The antidote was a bright green liquid, supposedly herbal, so they'd shredded lettuce into it. I had to lie motionless on the floor while they poured it into my mouth, so there I lay with a bit of lettuce across my top lip. Inevitably I started to quiver with the giggles and in the end I just exploded, splattering everyone with this vast gale of green lettuce liquid. It was awful.'

There was worse. A stunt-woman had been hired to stand in for Elspeth in a scene where her legs were tied and rats crawled up them. But as soon as the cameras were rolling and the first rat clambered on to the stunt-woman's foot she began yelling hysterically to the rat-handler to get them off, and as soon as her legs were untied she ran from the studio. No one else was available, so Elspeth herself agreed to the torture. 'I felt the rats' clawed feet crawling on to my legs,

clenched my teeth and tried not to panic. After about twenty seconds I could bear it no longer and said in a very high-pitched voice: "Get them off!" I was never so delighted to finish a scene.'

Elspeth wore out four uniforms during the series and never imagined she would step into the dreadful grey suit again. But after several successful theatre tours, a children's television series and making several commercials Elspeth was delighted to be asked to appear as Meg in the first *Prisoner: Cell Block H* stage-tour in Britain in the autumn of 1989. There was no problem about leaving her now grown sons, one at university and one in horticultural college. 'It was a fabulous adventure coming to Britain. I couldn't get over the devotion of the fans,' she said.

PATSY KING received a telephone call from Reg Watson: 'How tall are you, Patsy?' Like any bright actress she answered: 'How tall do you want me to be?' Finally she admitted she was only five feet three, hardly an imposing height for Wentworth's supposedly superior head officer. They had a solution: high heels and a piled-up hairstyle. It got her the part of the remote and not very efficient Erica Davidson but also made her the most dolled-up governor in the history of the prison services.

'But it has meant that every time I meet fans of the series they say, "Oh, aren't you short!",' said Patsy. But the classically trained actress, who'd played a host of serious heroines, had no hesitation about taking on the austere 'Davo' role when she read the scripts. 'I liked her, she

developed a lot. She was a bit of a mystery but told Lizzie something of her background which helped me understand her. She said she'd been a rebel at university but became a barrister; and her father, who was a judge, had fixed things for her, so she hadn't come up through the ranks. She didn't have that experience of dealing with people, which is why she made mistakes.' Patsy didn't need to be asked if there were funny moments inside Wentworth.

'Erica had a husband, played by Michael Cole. We saw him sitting in a restaurant, and he must still be there, covered in cobwebs,' she laughed. 'And there was a niece who came into prison on drugs charges. Erica's life was certainly action-packed. She was almost sacked twice, she almost resigned twice, she was

kidnapped and they threatened to cut off her fingers but luckily only got so far as cutting off her hair. In fact that sequence was a hoot. I was supposed to be being chased but we had to do the scenes again and again. I kept running too fast and the kidnappers couldn't catch me.'

But that wasn't Patsy's stickiest moment. Being shot was desperately uncomfortable. It was the scene which was to be the end-of-the-year cliffhanger: gun-fire, then Erica falling in slow motion, cutting to a close-up of her on the ground with blood running down from one arm.

'It meant I had to lie on the ground for about half an hour while they filmed me absolutely still,' she said. 'They gave me a pillow, so I wasn't in pain, but the "blood" was a mixture of raspberry and chocolate sauce which looked very realistic and dripped at the right speed. The trouble was that all the ants in the area smelt this wonderful sweet smell and came charging, attacking my arm.'

A scene where Davo was almost burnt alive, apparently stuck in a broom-cupboard, unable to unlock the door when fire broke out, was also tricky – and hilarious. 'I was supposed to tug at the door-handle to discover that the door wouldn't open. It wouldn't – because the handle came away in my hand. The cupboard was full of smoke – because we had an ice-machine in there. But we had to clear it and try again – and again the handle came off. I was really in hysterics, but of laughter not of terror.'

Patsy, who is single and lives in her home town of Melbourne, had had as wide a variety of roles as could be before *Prisoner*. She played Kate Andrews in the old soap *Bellbird* with Elspeth Ballantyne. Sheila Florance had played her mother in *Romanoff and Juliet* on stage, she'd toured Australia as Bubba in Ray Lawler's *Summer of the Seventeenth Doll* and she'd played Miss Behaviour in the children's television series *Adventure Island* as well as being much in demand on radio for 'young girl' voices because of her light voice. She left *Prisoner* after four and a half years because she felt she need a change, but came back towards the end of the series when the script had the replacement governor, Anne Reynolds, in difficulty with the tough warder nicknamed 'The Freak'.

'Erica stands out as a highspot in my career,' she reflected. 'After *Prisoner*, I played the Mother Superior in *Agnes of God*, a role that was also very important to me. But I suppose the two couldn't be more different.' When the chance came to re-create the role for the British stage- tour, Patsy was delighted to accept. 'It was very exciting to be in England in all those beautiful theatres,' she said. But the trip was marred by a health scare, she revealed. Patsy had to borrow some of Erica's courage and self-control. For a while she wondered if she'd played her last role. 'I discovered a tumour in my tummy while I was here, which was very worrying,' she said. 'I didn't want to do anything until I was home. Luckily when I got back I went to hospital and had an operation and the lump was benign. I'm absolutely fine now.'

VAL LEHMAN admits to such crimes as leaving one of her babies in a supermarket and on another occasion leaving her elder daughter in a public toilet and not noticing for ten minutes. She still feels guilty about it, but never, as her character Bea Smith felt about her kids, murderous. In fact Val hopes that the only thing the two women have in common is red hair and a throaty voice.

'Bea was tough but very motherly,' she said. 'She may have been a baddie, but the audience thought she was a goodie because she bucked the system and had a strong sense of justice. Everybody would like to punch authority in the nose and, because Bea did, people liked her.'

Born in Perth, Western Australia, Val's first ambition was to be an opera singer, but her too-deep voice put paid to that. She began a fine arts course, worked in student theatre, both acting and writing but left to marry an army officer at 19 and didn't start acting seriously until she was nearly 30, the mother of two girls and a boy, and had been posted with her husband to the Royal Military College of Science in Shrivenham, Berkshire. There she rode with the gentry on the White Horse and Old Berkshire Hunt during the day and was roped into amateur dramatics in the evenings. Her marriage was the price she paid for her determination to succeed as an actor.

Back in Australia she began working in the theatre, in musical comedy and in television. And she worked long and hard because she had three children to support. She, too, was in *Bellbird* – 'I was the TV lady who gave birth in the front seat of a

VW,' she said – and several other small roles. Then the role of Bea Smith, Wentworth's She Who Must Be Obeyed, came her way, a role which won her three 'Logie' awards and made her an internationally known star.

But the work was far from glamorous. The hours were long, often 14 hours for Val, and the scenes sometimes weird. Once, to keep the continuity correct, she had to lie for an hour early one morning in a pool of 'blood'. But there were small bonuses. Both her daughters appeared in the series. Joanne (now 24) played a young girl Bea met while on the run (and who dobbed her in) and Cassandra, 26, played Bea's daughter Debbie, drug-ridden and confused. This was a story-line Val supported wholeheartedly. Keenly aware of the drug problem in the Melbourne community at the time, she helped raise funds for a Drug Elimination Group. She also became the cast's Equity representative and worked for better pay and conditions. Val was, however, allowed 'parole' to appear as flashy Big Lil, a speakeasy operator, in the film *Kitty and the Bagman* and took a small part in another movie, *Mad Dog Morgan.*

Then, in March 1983, after four and a half years in *Prisoner*, she decided to 'escape'. She was offered a role in a play about a defiant girl wrestler, *Trafford Tanzi*, staged by Wilton Morley, son of Robert. She'd have been a fool, she said at the time, to turn the chance down. She admitted later that she feared being typecast if she'd stayed longer as tough old Bea. Several theatre and film roles followed but, although she was offered the chance to re-create Bea in the British stage-tour, she refused. She did come to Britain last year, though, and in triumph. She was mobbed and fêted during personal appearances and praised for her performance in the play *Summer of the Seventeenth Doll.*

She also married British radio journalist Charles Collins, 16 years her junior, something which did not endear her to some of the gay fans of *Prisoner*. Val pointed out that neither she nor Bea had been attracted to women and revealed that at one stage she had suggested a gay relationship for Bea to the producers. 'Bea had been in captivity for so long I thought something would have to give, but they said no – they wanted to keep her as a sort of mother figure. The poor woman must have been so frustrated!'

FIONA SPENCE made Vera 'Vinegar Tits' Bennett the most hated woman on the box, but the producers of *Prisoner* had taken a gamble casting her in the role. Unlike most of the leading performers, who had years of experience behind them, Fiona had graduated from a drama course only 18 months earlier and, apart from a role in the Aussie school soap *Glenview High*, had no grounding in television. But the risk paid off.

Luckily Vera's scragged-back hair – she wore it in a tight bun which she feared would eventually drop off – meant Fiona could escape being hissed at in the street. People never recognised her with her hair loose. 'One night I was at the movies with Elspeth Ballantyne,' she recalled. 'An avid viewer congratulated Elspeth on her performance and asked me whether I watched the series.'

Fiona was both grateful for the chance and delighted when Reg Watson decided to extend Vera's originally short life. 'Vera was lonely and didn't have anything in her life but prison work. When she tried to socialise it ended in disaster. I think that was part of her appeal. People can relate to loneliness. They feel sorry for her.'

Born in Kent to an Irish mother and an Australian surgeon father, she moved to Hong Kong at three and then at six to Oz. She describes her early life as not particularly serious. 'I was only interested in having a good time. I worked for a firm of architects, then decided that wasn't for me and moved to Canada to live for a year.' In her late twenties she lived in London and took a job in the casual dress department of Fortnum & Mason, the

posh Piccadilly store noted for its food department. 'I saw some stunning plays in the West End and great performers including Maggie Smith, Robert Stephens, Judi Dench and Albert Finney, and this seed was planted in my mind. I thought: This is ridiculous – I can't just *think* about it. I have to see if I can do it. And I've been doing it ever since.'

She is particularly fond of animals and keeps three King Charles spaniels, Strumpet, Scarlet and Spencer, at her Melbourne home. It's ironic because in one *Prisoner* episode the women found a stray spaniel, named it Prudence, shampooed and cosseted it, only to have Vera insist it must be sent to the RSPCA where it would probably be put down.

Unlike Vera and her later soap character, gossipy Celia in *Home And Away* she isn't a frump. She loves buying glamorous clothes and dressing up. But, like both Vera and Celia, Fiona is unmarried. 'I was engaged twice when I was 22 and 32 but decided it wasn't quite right for me,' she told reporter Gil Martin.

GLENDA LINSCOTT wanted to learn about prison life before she took on the role of unmarried mum Rita Connors who became Wentworth's top dog – or should that be bitch? – thorn in the side of Joan 'The Freak' Ferguson for the final 15 months of *Prisoner: Cell Block H*. The prisoners she visited were aggressively determined to tell her nothing but in fact revealed a great deal about their suspicions and anger. Without knowing, they must have helped, because Glenda won the 1986 Best Actress prize in the Penguin Awards. These tend to be rated more highly than the Logie Awards, because they are chosen by people inside the television industry.

Glenda told the *Weekly News*: 'I was granted permission to visit a prison and toured with the deputy governess. But in those circumstances the prisoners were on their best behaviour – which wasn't what I'd come to see.' She wanted to speak to the inmates without a figure of authority looming over them.

'To achieve this I offered to conduct a drama workshop in the prison. Around fifteen women attended, but unknown to me the workshop had been offered to them as some kind of reward for good behaviour. When I walked in the women had their arms folded and were glaring at me with real loathing. They were convinced I was a screw and demanded to know why I was pretending to be an actress and what I'd been sent to find out. Their faces were set like concrete – it was really quite frightening.'

Glenda revealed that *Prisoner* had given her career the boost it needed. When she left drama school she discovered that her height – six feet one inch – was a handicap at auditions. But for this soap women didn't have to fit into a 'Barbie Doll' mould.

When Glenda was living in Britain last year – her radio-director husband was completing an assignment for the BBC – *Prisoner* again rescued her career from a quiet patch. She'd feared she would not find work, but the first *Prisoner: Cell Block H* stage-tour was being mounted and the organisers heard from Australia that she was in Britain. She was thrilled to join the cast.

Interviewed about the appeal of the series, Glenda told *The Guardian*: 'Every story-line is around women incarcerated within four walls and not wanting to be there. I think that becomes a metaphor for all sorts of situations. It could be a housewife trapped at home, it could be gay people feeling trapped within their own sexuality. People identify with the metaphor.'

If BETTY BOBBITT had been able to look and sound a bit tougher, Bea Smith wouldn't have been a redhead and would have yelled with a Philadelphia accent. For American-born Betty, who'd gone Down Under in the sixties on a whim and had worked doing comedy on the fledgling Channel Seven television station, tested for the Bea role but was told she was too nice to be beastly Bea. Val Lehman won the role and, undaunted, Betty went back to work in the Australian theatre believing she'd heard the last of Wentworth Detention Centre. A year later, however, Grundy's producers called her again and asked her to test for one Judy Bryant, helpfully an American by birth, an inmate with an unhappy gay relationship in her past and one unlikely to serve a long sentence as she had a weak heart and would probably conk out after a few appearances.

Four years later Betty was still playing the snappy but soft-centred crim who was so well liked the scriptwriters gave her a pacemaker and pronounced her fit to suffer another unhappy affair – this time with Sharon Gilmore for whom she had deliberately gone to gaol.

Betty was told that Judy was a very tough 'bull-dyke', but the actress decided to add an edge of vulnerability which she thought fitted with Judy's self-sacrificing nature. 'I loved her; she was a victim of her love,' she said. But Betty revealed in an interview for *Gay Times* that the censors stepped in to 'play down' Judy's lesbianism.

'When they put my character in they specifically wanted her to be a lesbian but still fit within the censor's rules, although Australia's very much more liberal than England or America. So in the beginning she was allowed to be obviously in love and allowed to talk about it. Then the show was sold to America. At one point Judy had to kiss another character, and the Americans said, "No way! She can talk about it, but we don't want to see her kiss someone" . So from that moment on they decided to give Judy's gayness a low profile. We also had a new producer around that time, and he was very nervous about it, so I had to do more with *looks*!'

Betty is full of praise for the *Prisoner* production team, especially many of the extras who decided they would act gay and would stand in the background holding hands, half-jokingly ad-libbing such lines as 'You were great last night, honey!' Viewers never heard them, but the remarks served to support the actresses who were trying to make lesbian scenes work. But she was concerned at times that there was too much violence in the show. She told *Gay Times*: 'I was often upset because, you know, one week you'd be raped and the next you'd be at someone with a bit of lead pipe. And you'd think, "God, life is too hard".' Betty was one of the actresses Ian Smith mentioned who visited schools talking to teenagers who identified with *Prisoner* characters and were sometimes convinced that prison life was about cosy companionship. 'I had to tell them that we were just actors and that people who beat each other up go to gaol or lead horrible lives or raise miserable children.'

Betty now devotes her time to writing and directing for the stage and the cinema.

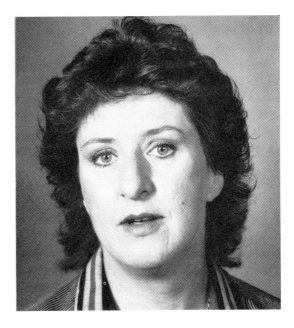

When big actress LESLEY BAKER came into Wentworth to play morose Monica Ferguson, the new 'standover' inmate when Bea Smith was temporarily off the premises, Australian viewers waited for the laughs. For Lesley was well known as one of television's popular comedy performers, a resident singer-comedienne on the *In Melbourne Tonight* show, a favourite on 'The Paul Hogan Show' and many other light entertainment series. She also had her own morning show for a time. She had been trying to move into straight drama and had taken several small roles. 'I started off as a nymphomaniac lady garage mechanic, then graduated to junior prostitutes and madames. The gangster's wife has been one of my specialities, too,'

she said. She was thrilled to be offered the Big Monnie role in *Prisoner* – she joked that she felt Monnie really loved little Fred but he had to be bashed because he kept putting his hand in the till – and moved into Wentworth on a short-term contract that was extended when the character became popular.

But her 'sentence' was to be cut short by a personal tragedy. Behind Monnie's aggression was the actress's worry about her toddler son Benjamin whom she was bringing up alone following a separation from her husband. She had suspected there could be a problem, but it was only when he was examined by doctors at 10 months that brain damage, suffered at birth, was diagnosed. Lesley felt the child needed her constant attention and dedication and consequently gave up her *Prisoner* role.

Some years later the producers tried to

tempt her back, offering her the role of a new character, Tinkerbell, a tough bikie who sheltered an escapee. But Lesley declined. These days Ben is able to go to school and Lesley is able to take on stage work, and this year performed at a theatre restaurant owned by actor Terry Gill who played Inspector Grace in *Prisoner*.

ANNE HADDY now plays soap's nicest and wisest granny, Helen Daniels in *Neighbours*, and it's hard to think of her as a snobbish old baggage. But she was certainly unpleasant in her role as Alice Hemmings, Doreen's terminally ill mother in *Prisoner*. When Alice went into a coma and died few tears must have been shed. In fact Alice's last weeks were an anxious time for everyone who knew Anne. Previously healthy, she'd suffered a heart attack in March 1979 – ironically after completing a season in a play called *Bodies* – and had planned major surgery, four bypass operations to relieve blocked arteries, later in the year. She was well enough, though, to undertake the *Prisoner* role before the operation and welcomed the not-too-strenuous work as a way of taking her mind off her heart. But a technicians' dispute delayed work at the Melbourne studios, and Anne flew back to her Sydney home. By the time the dispute was settled Anne was only days away from the scheduled operation. She had to fly back to Melbourne to complete her scenes with Colette Mann, who played her daughter. 'The cast and crew were marvellous,' Anne recalled. 'The wardrobe ladies would fuss over me and keep me well rugged up while I was on location to make sure I didn't suffer any bad chest-pains. And, as the role called for Alice's cancer to become more serious and for her to slow down through weakness, I was slowing down myself. By then I was feeling the need.' A couple of years later Anne, too, suffered cancer, of the stomach, underwent more surgery, completed her role as Rosie in *Sons and Daughters* and, to round things off, went back to hospital for surgery for a broken hip. When her *Neighbours* character Helen Daniels collapsed with a stroke on television this year no one could have doubted she'd fight back and recover!

PEITA TOPPANO was getting tired of the way actresses tended to be treated – usually cast in passive roles – and photographed looking sweet, in bikinis or in 'girlie' poses, when along came the offer to play Karen Travers, a woman who'd murdered her husband after he forced her to have an abortion. It sounded 'gutsy', she said, and the fact that most of the roles were for women was exciting. But there were to be a few token men, she discovered when rehearsals began and she chatted to the show's creator, Reg Watson. One role was the Wentworth doctor, and she suggested English actor Barry Quin whom she'd met when he'd toured Australia with a production of *Othello* and she was on stage in *A Chorus Line*. Barry, who'd returned to England, sent a cassette of his work to Watson and later flew back to take the role. The couple, unhappily in love in the series, married a few weeks after the series went to air. In *Prisoner* Karen and Dr Miller's university romance was slowly rekindled. Sadly Peita and Barry's marriage is now over.

Born in London, Peita came from a musical family and hoped to be a classical dancer. A fall down some steps which broke a bone in a foot put paid to that, so she concentrated on singing, appearing in most of Australia's musical television shows as well as in *The Young Doctors* in which she played Dr Gail Henderson. Her role as the black-hearted villainess in *Return to Eden* and the vamp in *Fields of Fire II* brought her further success in Britain. Later in 1990 she appears in the ITV mini-series *The Paper Man*.

MAGGIE KIRKPATRICK has no regrets about her time as Joan 'The Freak' Ferguson, the 'nasty' who came in when 'Vinegar' Vera left. 'It sounds odd to say I enjoyed Joan – she was hideous, a sadistic, corrupt lesbian,' she told me. 'But I did, for nearly five hundred episodes. I certainly didn't mind playing a lesbian, because I felt quite safe in my own sexuality. Also I saw her as a shy, ugly woman, not the predatory monster who'd attack 16-year-old girls. When she fell in love, it weakened her, and the younger woman, who'd been attracted to her toughness, promptly went off her.

'Most people hated her – that was the idea; I found it very gratifying. It showed you shouldn't underestimate the audience.' The hardest time for Maggie was when The Freak was supposed to be suffering from a brain injury after being knocked unconscious by a prisoner. 'It was difficult because every now and then Joan would be in mid-sentence and all of a sudden she would "vague -off" because she was getting these awful headaches. In the end I *was* getting headaches, because I had to concentrate so hard,' she said. Joan was carted off for brain surgery. Maggie took a holiday in Paris with her actor friend John Hargreaves. When she returned she recorded a song-and-dance number for an Australia Day concert. 'After a long stretch as the Freak, it was great to be a girl again,' she joked.

When *Prisoner* ended, Maggie went back to the theatre, and in 1988 was delighted to take on Ivy Hackett, self-styled Duchess of the short-lived soap *Richmond Hill*. 'She liked getting her own way, too, but that's all Ivy had in common with the Freak. I had a lot of fun with her,' said Maggie.

KERRY ARMSTRONG didn't have to act one of Lyn 'The Wonk' Warner's wobblier moments. When Lyn was supposed to have had an accident which left her on crutches for a few days, Kerry actually needed the crutches. She had been playing tennis, partnering Barry Quin who played Dr Greg Miller against a couple of the station's newsmen. She fell and tore two tendons. At the hospital it was a case of 'Oh no, you again!' For Kerry was as prone to sporting injuries as the Wonk was prone to disasters. Kerry had countless fingers broken in softball, a spinal injury from tobogganing, and a variety of leg injuries from surfing and horse-riding. Happily it hadn't slowed her career. As a 15-year-old schoolgirl she toured with British comedy actor Sid James, then took

than the one they'd known in their Glasgow tenement. As a boy soprano he sang with the local symphony orchestra and gradually edged his way into showbusiness through radio work, newsreading and as host of the Australian version of the children's show 'Crackerjack'. 'I had to cross Leslie Crowther's name off the script and substitute my own,' he recalled, chuckling. In 1972 he returned to Britain and won roles in numerous television shows including *Z-Cars* and *General Hospital*, in which he played a brilliant doctor with a drink problem. But his career here was interrupted in 1979 when the deadline for those Australians wishing to retain their citizenship was drawing nigh. He and his Australian wife Kay and their two children dashed back to register in the nick of time.

a job as GTV-9's weather girl before landing roles in television series including *Cop Shop* and *The Sullivans*. For the role of Lyn, Kerry spent several weeks talking to inmates of Fairlea prison. To cry convincingly, as Lyn the Wonk did often, Kerry said she forced herself to imagine terrible accidents had befallen her family. Kerry went on to work briefly in *Dynasty* in America.

JAMES SMILLIE landed in Wentworth Detention Centre after being 'repatriated' to Australia, rather like one of those Victorian criminals shipped from Britain out to Oz. Unlike the convicts, James was grateful and looks back fondly to his time 'inside'. He explains that he emigrated to Perth in Western Australia as a child when his family were searching for a better life

But he discovered that work opportunities there were few and far between.

'Then I landed a thirteen-week contract with "*Prisoner*" playing Steve Wilson the lawyer and it was the best set I've ever worked on,' he said. 'Apart from me and Barry Quin, the rest of the cast were women and I've never been in a less bitchy atmosphere. We had many laughs and I made some true friends.'

In 1980, James came back to Britain to star in the musical about Barnardo with Fiona Fullerton and a cast of 20 youngsters playing small vagabonds. It was with his role as the miracle-working surgeon Dan Marshall, the man who rebuilt actress Rebecca Gilling's face after she was mauled by a crocodile, in the mini-series *Return to Eden* that James became best-known to British viewers. The series co-starred his pal Peita Toppano, the girl he loved and lost in *Prisoner*, who played his enemy here.

While he was back in Australia filming *Eden*, *Prisoner* was ending its run and James was surprised to be contacted with an offer to return to Wentworth in a new role. He turned it down believing it would be insulting to the show's loyal followers, who would certainly remember Steve Wilson. So it was back to London again for the Smillie family and for James the most exciting singing role so far, taking over the lead role from Denis Quilley in the musical about the comic agonies in a French gay club, *La Cage Aux Folles,* at the Palladium. Anti-AIDS sentiment sweeping the country at the time led to the show's early closure, but James went on to star in the prestigious production of *Kiss Me Kate.* Working with members of the Royal Shakespeare Company made James a strong defender of soap. 'Some of the best actors I know started out in *Prisoner*,' he declared.

4
THE CAPTIVE AUDIENCE

WATCHING *PRISONER* FROM THE INSIDE

'I laughed when I first saw *Prisoner: Cell Block H*, but I also cried because it made me remember things,' said Chris Tchaikovsky, a former Holloway inmate, now director of the welfare and campaigning group Women In Prison.

'I'd known about it for some time, because lots of ex-prisoners and other people I'd met talked about it. I don't think women can actually watch it inside, because it's on too late and there aren't many chances to video things. I didn't actually watch it myself until I had to attend a Youth Section meeting and I knew I'd be asked about it. It does what no other programme does, and that's show lesbians as part of society, just *there*. As to whether it's true to life – well, all I can say is that I could match those crazy incidents with things I know have happened. Yes, there are escape-attempts – a woman walked out of Holloway last Christmas despite all the security there. There are stunts. One is called "changing", where a prisoner changes places with a remand prisoner and goes out when the release comes; then the switch is reported, and of course the real remand prisoner has to be let out. There are silly pranks – Mars bars being passed along the lines in church, exploding packages, fights. Yes, there are affairs between inmates, and between inmates and officers. There are what're called "con-lovers" – warders who are soft on certain prisoners – and officers do sometimes get the sack for it. And, yes, there are sadistic warders. Remember, about eighty per cent of prison officers in this country are closet lesbians; they can't "come out" about it, they can't go to gay clubs for fear of running into ex-prisoners who would tell, so they lead very insular, sad lives. That inevitably means a few of them become nasty like Vera Bennett. And lesbian activities between prisoners are still banned. I don't mean the whole going-to-bed bit – just holding hands. In Styal prison in Manchester only the other week they put a couple of women on charges for lesbian activities. Imagine: some big butch officer reprimanding two inmates for doing what she'd like to do – hold hands. And there are also male officers who can peer in at women at any time during the twenty-four hours – when they're on the toilet, in the shower, in bed. It's horrific.'

Despite what Chris feels is the over-all daftness of *Prisoner: Cell Block H*, she thinks it's preferable to the British series about women inside, *Within These Walls*, which ITV began showing in 1974. 'There you'd see Googie Withers done up to the nines as the governor talking to some new arrival, who'd be crying because her pussycat hadn't been fed. And in the next scene you'd see Googie going to the woman's flat and stroking the cat. Ludicrous! I can only tell you that if *Prisoner: Cell Block H* were shown at seven-thirty in the evening every inmate and officer in British prisons would be riveted. It would shoot ahead of *Coronation Street*.'

Picture page 84 Members of the cast of the stage play

Prison officer Jackie Mobbs, who is also a spokeswoman for the Prison Officers' Association, agrees with Chris. 'I was given some free tickets to the stage-show of *Prisoner*, and I took some of them to Holloway, and the reaction was amazing. The officers were very keen indeed. I went to see the play, and I watched an episode or two. I thought it was hilarious – and I'm being kind saying that.'

Before Jackie worked in this country as a prison officer she worked at a woman's prison in Australia which might well have served as the model for *Prisoner*. 'It was a very small place then, and I found it very corrupt. The officers did not have the best sort of rapport with inmates that we try to have here. In my opinion there were more professional criminals in Australia than here, too. Here many of the women inside are just inadequate; there they were really tough.'

THE FAN CLUB

Spiky-haired Ros Vecsey and Tracey Elliott reckon they look like a couple of hard nuts. In fact they looked like inmates of Wentworth Detention Centre before they'd even heard of it or *Prisoner: Cell Block H*. 'Normally, at the sight of us, old ladies would cross the street,' laughed Ros. 'Instead they now tend to send us tenners at Christmas to buy ourselves a drink in thanks for what we've done.'

Ros and Tracey always send back the money. But they're glad someone appreciates the labours which began one Saturday in 1987 when they came home from the pub, switched on the television and happened to catch a gang of tough Aussie women in denim.

The two Derby girls, unemployed then as now, thought it screamingly funny. In future weeks they noticed that people were leaving their local early especially to get home in time for *Prisoner*, too. 'It was ruining our social life,' joked Ros, now twenty-six, who'd previously thought *Sons and Daughters* was the biggest hoot. 'We thought: If this show is so popular at street-level with all these sorts of people – greasy bikers, little old ladies, the lot – why don't we start a fan club?'

Next step was a five-minute interview on a regional television-show, *Central Post*, presented by Anna Soubry, one Sunday. By the following Tuesday the girls had received 300 letters about the fan club – the encouragement they needed to publish their first newsletter, *The Phantom of the Soap Opera*, paid for partly out of their dole money and partly out of a legacy left to Tracey, also twenty-six, by her grandmother. The girls charged £4 a head subscription to the club and were inundated with requests to carry on. Membership flourished to the extent that the girls came off the dole and, hearing that Val Lehman, who played Bea Smith, wanted to visit Britain, secured a £40-a-week grant from the Government Enterprise Scheme to set up as her sole agent.

'It was wonderful,' said Ros. 'We did all sorts of personal appearances with Val, and wherever she went she was mobbed. The series certainly attracts a very diverse audience. We have middle-aged professional men who are fans, accountants and

Val Lehman flanked by Fan Club founders Tracey Elliott (left) and Ros Vecsey

solicitors as well as pensioners. And it has a very strong following among gay men. Val Lehman was mobbed by "queens" wanting to marry her,' she laughed. 'But many lesbians don't like *Prisoner*, because they feel it is not an accurate portrayal of lesbian life. And once it was sold to America there was hardly any lesbian stuff at all – no kissing, nothing below the waist.

The girls know that many viewers take the series at face value, caring about the characters and enjoying the stories just as they used to believe in *Crossroads*. 'We're not worried about those people,' said Ros.

'It's the men who write to us saying they love to wait till their wives go to bed, then they can put on her denim skirt and yellow blouse and watch *Prisoner: Cell Block H* – they're the ones who worry us.'

The girls know that the series has a huge following among gay men, for whom Wentworth is a high-camp camp. But despite Ros and Tracey's claims that they laugh at *Prisoner* they defend it stoutly, too, suggesting a deep affection. 'It's not just a gay cult, though,' says Ros. 'Our research shows there are about ten million viewers in Britain. It's way ahead of its time in terms of discussing controversial issues. *Coronation Street* only recently got round to discussing abortion, but *Prisoner* was dealing with incest and rape years ago. In some ways people treat it as the poor relation of Australian soaps, which is crazy. I used to like *Sons and Daughters* for its escapism, but I don't like *Neighbours*. If they pitched *Prisoner* against *Neighbours*, we know which would win.'

Along with many members of the fan club they were unhappy about the

The Mayor of Derby shares a joke with Sheila Florance, Val Lehman and Amanda Muggleton on their arrival at the civic reception.

Prisoner: Cell Block H stage-tour, concerned that it didn't genuinely reflect the character of the series.

Today Ros and Tracey are stars in their own right. Their newsletter, *The H-Block Herald*, is famous, and the term 'Blockies' for *Prisoner* fans has entered the language. But in a sense they have really become prisoners, too. 'Some of the fan club members are a bit extreme. We've had them turning up at the front door of Tracey's house and rushing across the street to touch us. We seem to be recognised everywhere – even in Sainsbury's,' said Ros.

Despite some earlier setbacks the fan club has gone from strength to strength. A successful tour with Betty Bobbitt at the beginning of 1990 was followed in September by their most ambitious project to date: the triumphant 'On the Outside' tour, with a show called *The Great Escape*. Ros says, 'We brought Amanda Muggleton and Sheila Florance over specially for the tour and Val, of course, was already working here. The response was amazing.' They were mobbed at the airport, given a reception by the Mayor of Derby, fêted by Wogan and the show itself was enthusiastically received. The girls worked with the producers Chrysalis Television to ensure that all these memorable events were captured on video.

The fan club can be contacted at
28 St James Chambers
St James Street, Derby DE1 1QZ

The Great Escape video, containing coverage of the show and behind the scenes footage of the tour is available for £14.99 plus £1 postage and packing. Cheques and postal orders should be made payable to the Great Escape Video Offer and sent to Eve Promotions, 28 St James Chambers, St James Street, Derby DE1 1QZ.

THE WOMEN OF WENTWORTH TREAD THE BRITISH BOARDS

Australia was just a faraway place to John Farrow and Lee Abbott, who run Alternative Plays, the company which first staged the cult musical *The Rocky Horror Show* in Britain. Then *Neighbours* became a smash-hit television-show, and John had the idea of negotiating to bring some of that show's actors to Britain to star in touring plays – a way of allowing those artists to show what else they could do and to attract new people to the theatre via television.

Peter O'Brien, famous as Shane from *Neighbours*, was the first to arrive – to tour in *Butterflies Are Free*. Others followed. Eight stars or former stars of the Ramsay Street saga will be coming to Britain at Christmas 1990 to work in pantomime or other productions, thanks to John.

Then someone mentioned *Prisoner: Cell Block H*. John remembered he had known Reg Watson distantly years ago when Reg worked in Birmingham on *Crossroads*. He contacted Reg, the faxes began to fly between London and Sydney, and the result was a stage-play based on the first six episodes of the television series written and delivered with the blessing of Grundy.

'We then began asking Australian actresses if they'd like to re-create their roles here, and many were very keen,' said

Lee, John's assistant. 'Elspeth Ballantyne, Glenda Linscott and Patsy King came in 1989, and Joanna Monro took over the Franky Doyle role. The actress who played Bea Smith was Brenda Longman, who used to be the voice of Sooty's girl-friend Soo – so it was a bit of a change!

'The show was just an amazing success. I think they were stunned by the response of the fans. The audience seemed to be made up of so many different types of people – blue-rinsed ladies, professional people, lots of people from the gay community. It was a very strange mix really. I went to watch the show in Wimbledon, and it was like a pantomime audience, lots of hissing and booing and clapping. It felt very exciting. Then I went to watch it in Hanley near Stoke-on-Trent, one of the areas where the series is shown two or three times a week and avidly followed,

and there was complete silent concentration. Obviously the audience were enjoying it as a straight drama.'

The success of the first thirteen-week tour led to a second tour with Fiona Spence and Jane Clifton, and again the box-office did well. In Glasgow and Liverpool the theatres were sold out. A third tour in the autumn was planned, and John and Lee travelled to Australia to sign up new stars. Maggie Kirkpatrick, who was having a great success in the musical *Anything Goes*, was the first to agree. John's untimely death meant the third tour was postponed until early 1991.

Ken Dodd saw one of the shows in Liverpool. 'I was tickled,' he said. 'It's not easy to bring people in who aren't used to the live shows. *Prisoner: Cell Block H* seems to be doing it, and I'm delighted. It's very good for British theatre.'

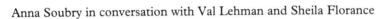

Anna Soubry in conversation with Val Lehman and Sheila Florance

CELEBRITY REVIEWS

Prisoner: Cell Block H is an 'in' show in showbusiness. Fans are said to include Dame Edna Everage and Ronnie Barker, comedian Julian Clary, disc jockeys Phil Sayer and Andy Kershaw, television presenter Phillip Schofield, pop singer Marc Almond, formerly of Soft Cell, and many more. Here is what some of them say.

Comedian Roy Hudd: 'I'm mad about it. I love Noelene Bourke – she's the prettiest. My wife Debbie does a great impression of her saying "Wot yer gonna do about it?" I think that's why I fell in love with her. I was amazed to find there's such a following. For Debbie's birthday treat I wanted to take her to the stage-show, but we couldn't get tickets.'

Keith Vaz, Leicester MP: 'I usually get round to signing all my papers at about midnight, and I always switch on *Prisoner: Cell Block H*, because life in Wentworth is so like life in the House of Commons it gets me in the mood. I'm a great fan of Bea Smith, and of course I follow what the Freak does. In many ways she reminds me of Margaret Thatcher.'

Jazz singer and art critic George Melly: 'It's the only soap I really watch, and I love it. I think it's because it brings out the lesbian in me.'

Terry Deal and Gillian Rodgerson of 'Gay Times' magazine: ' *Prisoner* stimulates the parts other soaps can't reach. And we especially like Miss Bennett. She keeps us off the streets on Thursday nights.'

Actor Leslie Grantham, former 'EastEnders' star: 'I now know why the inmates of Strangeways stayed on the roof. They were playing non-stop videos of *Prisoner: Cell Block H* downstairs.'

Broadcaster Nina Myskow: 'I adore it. Obviously the actresses took ugly-pills. Amazing how they all worked.'

Australian writer Kathy Lette: ' *Prisoner* is our revenge for all the high tack you Poms have exported Down Under.'

Rock singer Vicki from Fuzzbox: 'I like it because there is a really positive view of women in it. There's nobody with shoulderpads, or wearing tons of make-up or with glammy hairdos. It makes me laugh, but I'm addicted.'

Singer Ali Campbell of UB40: 'It's so over-the-top and unlike any other soap on TV. My favourite character is Bea Smith. I'd love the chance to play one of the screws and be a real bastard.'

Broadcaster Michael Parkinson: ' *Prisoner* is watched by two groups of people. One lot still think Elvis Presley is alive and working in a bar in Worthing. The others are lady sumo wrestlers.'

Chat-show host Jonathan Ross: 'There's that early-"Crossroads" quality about *Prisoner: Cell Block H*. I'm very taken by some of the women. But I'm kind of glad they're in captivity and in Australia.'

ROLL-CALL

LESLEY BAKER (Monica Ferguson) appeared in an early episode of 'The Flying Doctors' as *a mother of nine*.

CAROL BURNS (Franky Doyle) appeared in an episode of the British series *Hannay* in 1989.

ANNE CHARLESTON played three roles in *Prisoner* – Mum's daughter, a policewoman and Mrs Keen, mother of Rebecca Keen ('Red Keen') – before finding fame as Madge Ramsay in *Neighbours*.

STEFAN DENNIS played a juvenile runaway who hid in the roof of the house in which Doreen, during her tough period, was staying. He became close to Doreen and even kissed her. It was an experience about which he was most ungallant later, describing it as his 'worst moment' in the show. He went on to play the charmless would-be tycoon Paul Robinson in *Neighbours*.

GARY FILES (Fred Ferguson) reappeared as unreliable plumber Tom Ramsay in *Neighbours*.

VIVEAN GRAY appeared as Edna, in Wentworth for fraud, before achieving greater notoriety as Mrs Mangel in *Neighbours*.

ANNE HADDY rose again from the grave of Doreen's estranged mother to be reincarnated in *Neighbours* as the worthy Helen Daniels, mother-in-law of Jim Robinson, artistic patron of Spray-Can Nick and probably the greatest painter ever to immortalise the Bungle-Bungles on canvas.

KATE JACKSON (Martha Eves) turned up in Ramsay Street for a while as a doting Italian momma.

GERARD MAGUIRE (Jim Fletcher) changed sides for a couple of episodes of *Neighbours* when he tried to rob Des Clarke's bank, even holding a gun to Des's head.

RAY MEAGHER, nasty Nam veteran Geoff Butler, is currently every bit as unlovable in *Home and Away*.

AMANDA MUGGLETON (Chrissie Latham) went on to *Richmond Hill*.

TOM OLIVER (Ken Pearce) suddenly turned up in *Neighbours* as a millionaire car-dealer and briefly rivalled Harold Bishop for the hand of Madge Ramsay. He was given to prodding Harold in the belly and taunting him with recollections of the humiliations he had made Harold suffer at school. This eventually brought Harold as close to fisticuffs as he is ever likely to get.

ANNE SCOTT-PENDLEBURY, who appeared briefly in *Prisoner* as a former lover of Judith Bryant, achieved more lasting fame as prim and proper Hilary in *Neighbours*.

IAN SMITH (Ted Douglas) seems set to achieve immortality as portly Harold Bishop in *Neighbours*.

JAMES SMILLIE who played dashing lawyer Steve Wilson, reappeared as the equally dashing doctor in *Return to Eden*.

FIONA SPENCE (Vera Bennett) subsequently re-emerged in the highly successful *Home and Away*.

PEITA TOPPANO, who played the righteous Karen Travers, was next seen as the thoroughly unscrupulous villainess in *Return to Eden*.

ROWENA WALLACE, famous as Pat the Rat in 'Sons and Daughters', played Anne Griffin in *Prisoner*, inside on a robbery charge but found to be mentally unbalanced (or 'two sausages short of a barbi') and eventually sent to a psychiatric hospital.

MARY WARD ('Mum') appeared briefly in *Neighbours* as Mark Granger's protective (American) mother.

WENTWORTHSPEAK

arvo: afternoon

buckless: hopeless (as in 'You've a buckless chance of doing that)

buy-up: the weekly opportunity for the women to use their wages to buy cigarettes, biscuits and 'feminine items'; usually the first privilege to be withdrawn in the event of trouble

compo: compensation (i.e., for wrongful imprisonment)

curry: big trouble (as in 'You'll get curry for jobbing that cop')

buckless: as in you've a buckless chance of doing that – means hopeless

dag: frump

dill: idiot, half-wit, twit

dob [someone] in: betray, grass on

drongo: real dope, moron

giving me the irrits: getting on my nerves

the good oil: inside information, intelligence, lowdown

grog: booze (always illicit, usually home-made)

job: attack, work over (as in 'You'll get curry for jobbing that cop')

lag: inform the authorities; betray

have a lend of: string someone along, kid someone (as in 'I was just having a lend of you')

the pound: punishment section, where wayward prisoners are sent to spend time in solitary confinement

preggo: with child

Rack off! Clear off!

Ripper! Wonderful!

screws: prison officers

silvertails: the well-off, the well-connected, the privileged

smoko: (unauthorised) break from work for a cigarette

sprung: caught (as in 'Bourke pulled a swifty and got sprung')

sticky-beak: inquisitive person, Nosy Parker

stirrable: easily annoyed or teased

stumblebum: not succesful (e.g. Martha)

swifty: (as in 'pull a swifty') con, dodge, swindle, trick (the implication being that it is a swift and simple opportunist crime)

VJ: Visiting Justice - local magistrate brought in to try serious cases of indiscipline

Well, bugger me gently! You amaze me!

WENTWORTH WISDOM

VERA *(attempting to bring the prison drama group to order as they giggle over their attempt to come to terms with 'A Midsummer Night's Dream')*: It's not a comedy!

'Where's Bea?'
'She's in her cell writing a play.'

DOREEN: Did ya hear about the case of hepatitis they had in D Block?
MARGO: That lot'll drink anything!

MARGO *(to Noelene)*: Rack off, Hairy Legs!

LIZZIE *(on Martha Eves)*: She gets bigger every time I look at her. You'd need a pickaxe to get behind *her.*

JANET DOMINGUEZ *(recently arrived at the prison and feigning ignorance)*: Miss . . . Bent, isn't it?
VERA *(icily)*: Bennett.

LIANNE BOURKE *(explaining how - against all odds - she has managed to land a job as a checkout girl at the local supermarket)*: The manager couldn't take his eyes off me tits.

ANDREW REYNOLDS *(having informed the police that his assistant, Kay White, has absconded with the payroll)*: They're putting out a general description.
VINCE TALBOT: What of - her or the money?

DOREEN *(trying to convince herself that telling husband Kevin that she is expecting someone else's baby won't be all that difficult)*: All I have to say is that I got pregnant because I got raped. I don't have to go into details.
BEA: You've gotta expect a few questions, love.

JUDITH BRYANT *(on Vera Bennett)*: If I had a dog with a face like that, I think I'd shave its bum and teach it to walk backwards.